GREEN MAN

& GREEN WOMAN

COLORING BOOK

THIS BOOK BELONGS TO

....

ILLUSTRATED BY

ANTONY BRIGGS

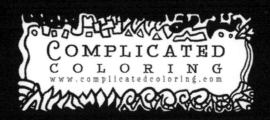

COMPLICATED
COLORING
www.complicatedcoloring.com

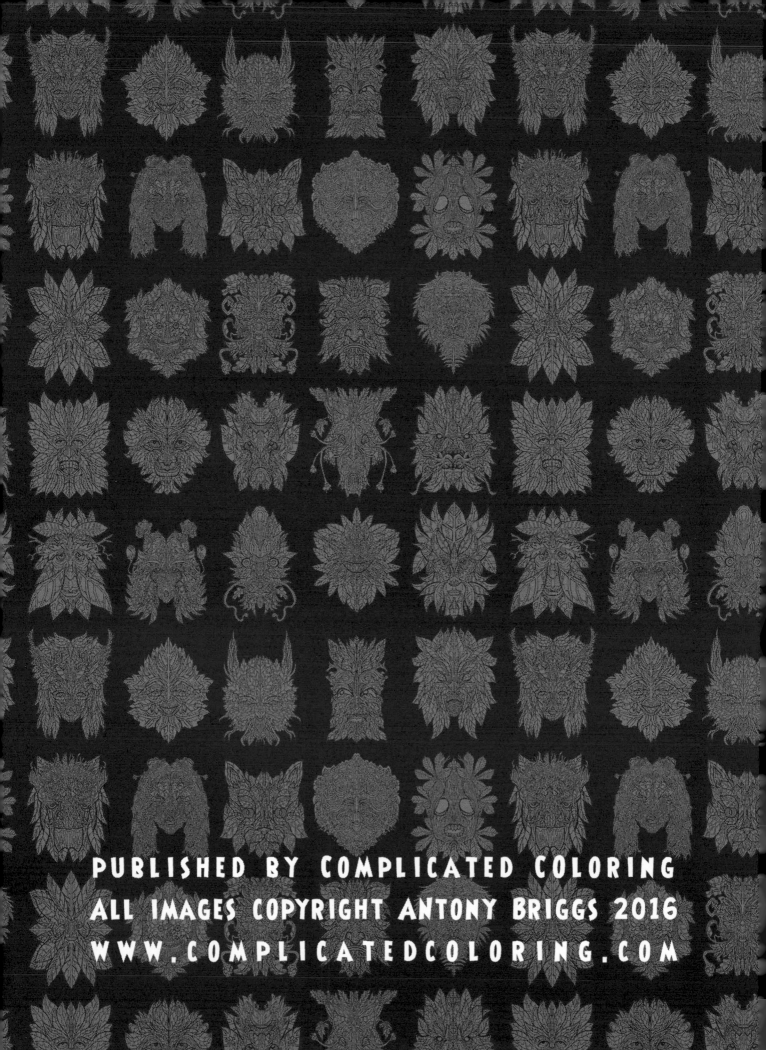

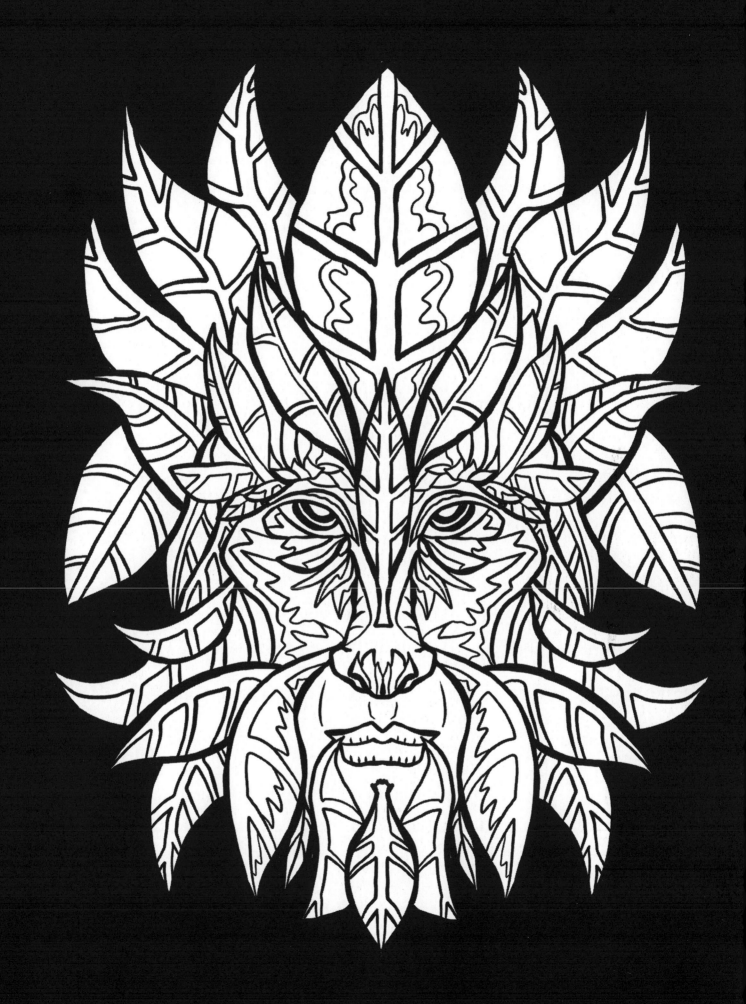

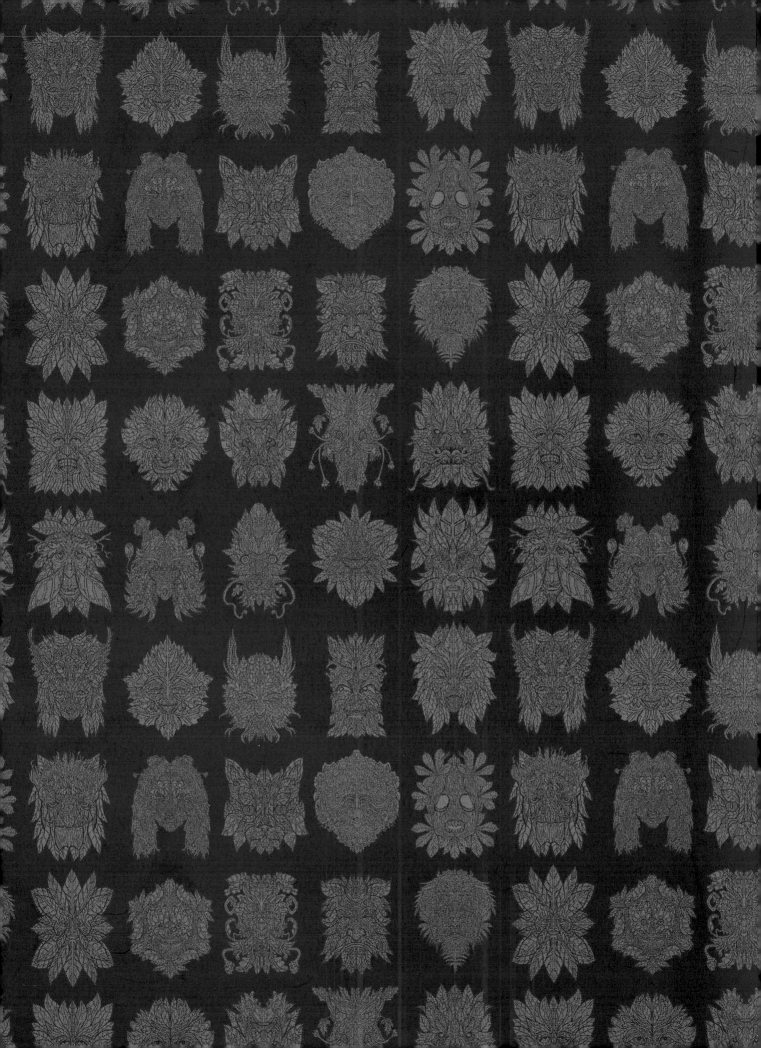

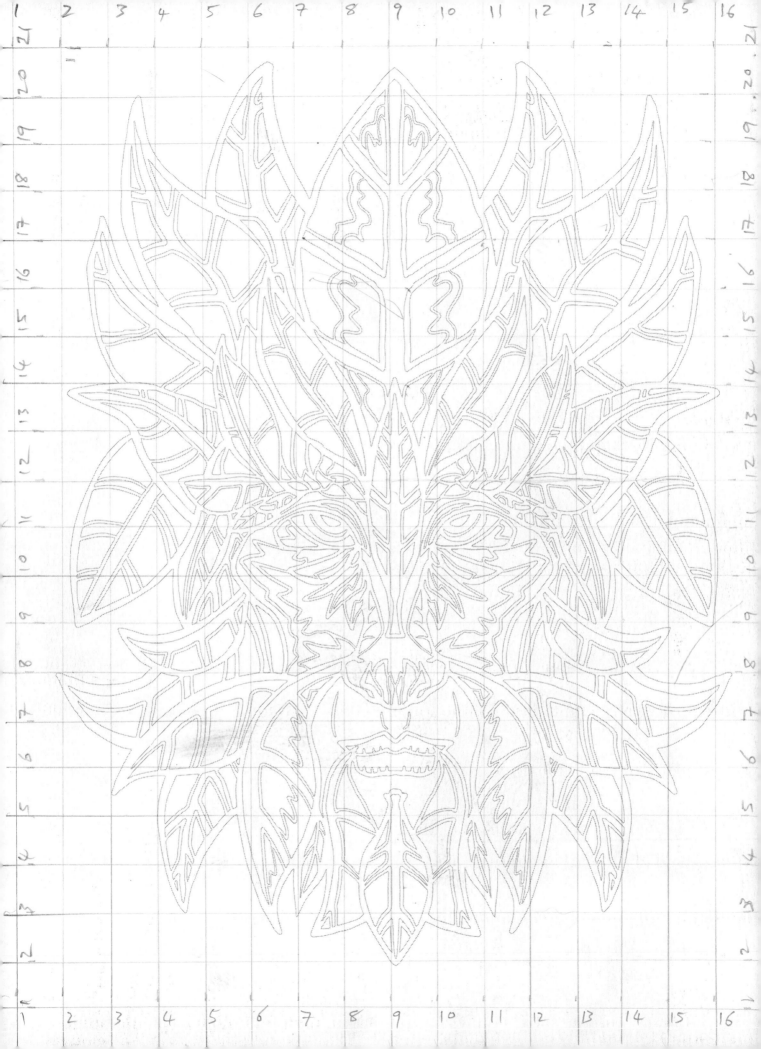

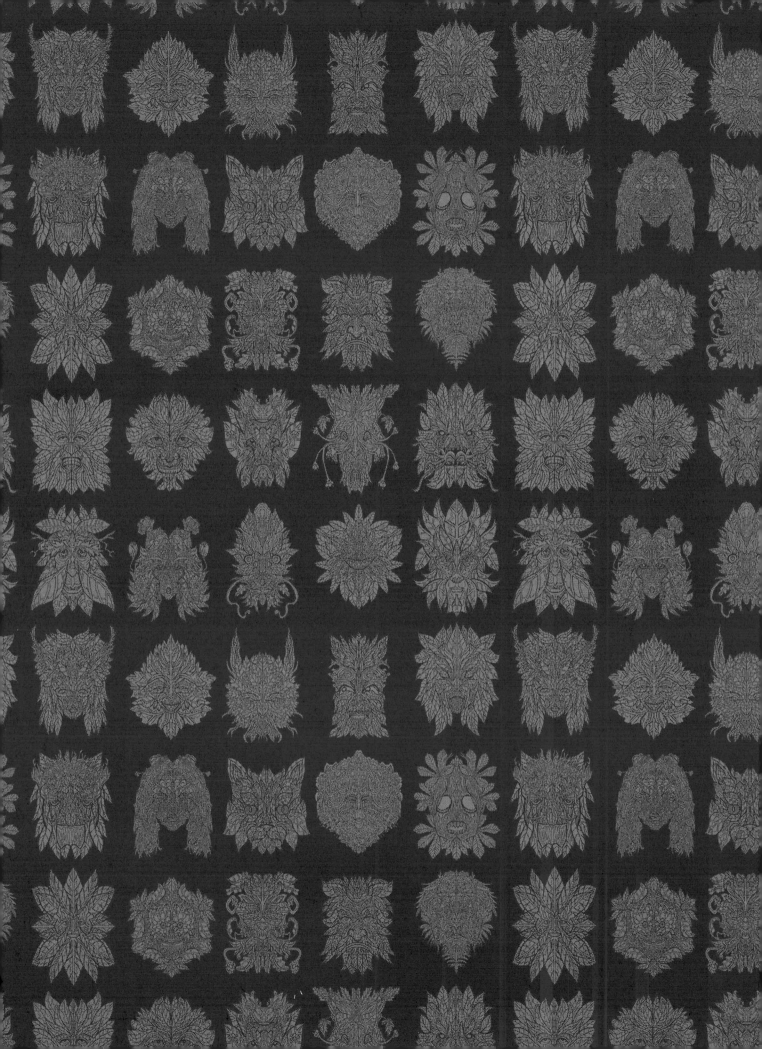

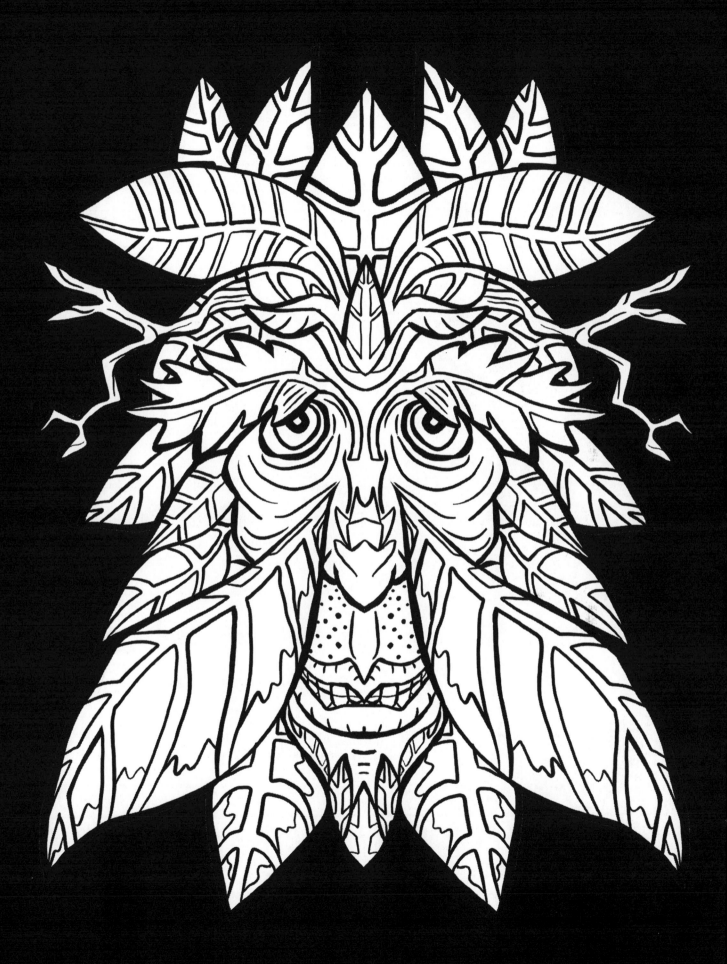

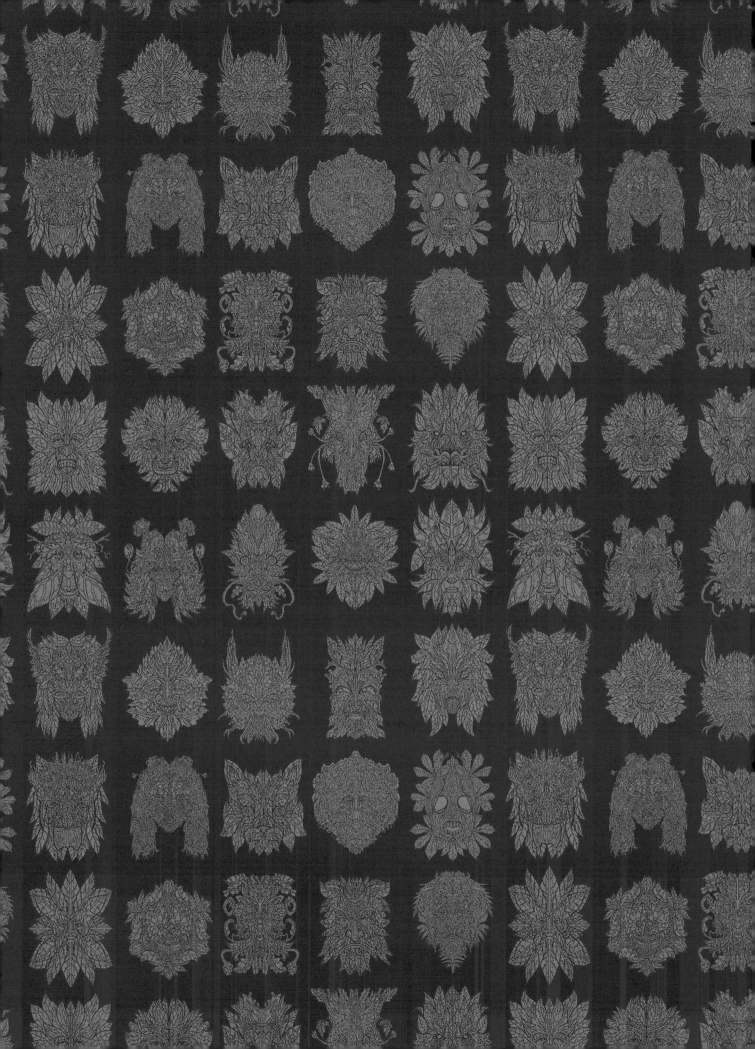

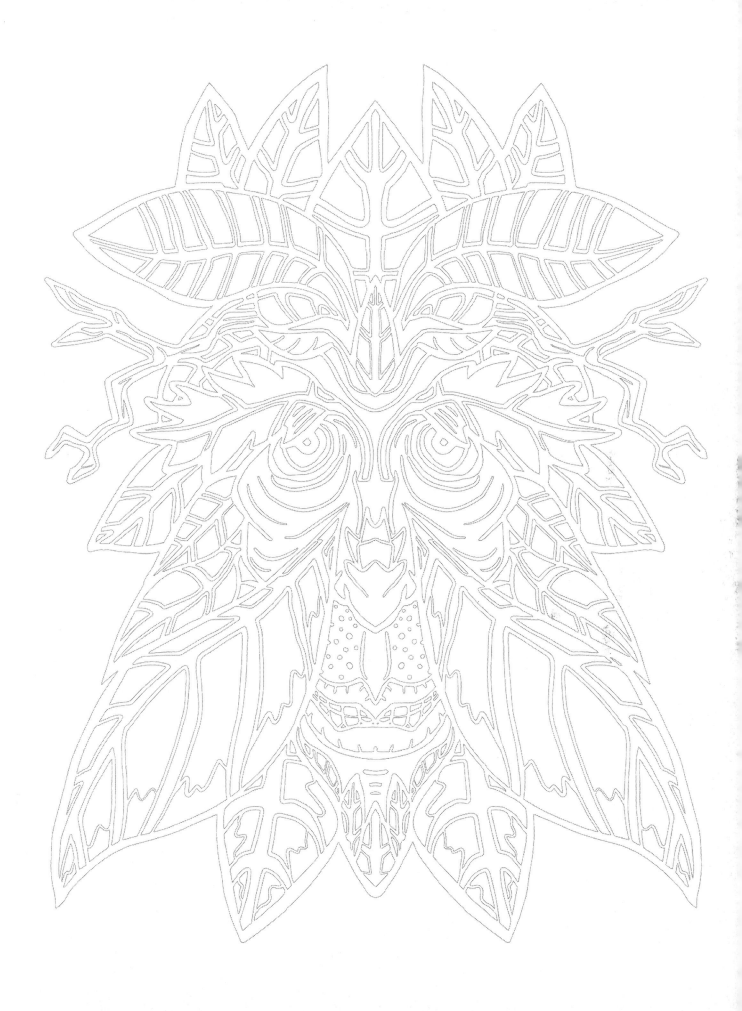

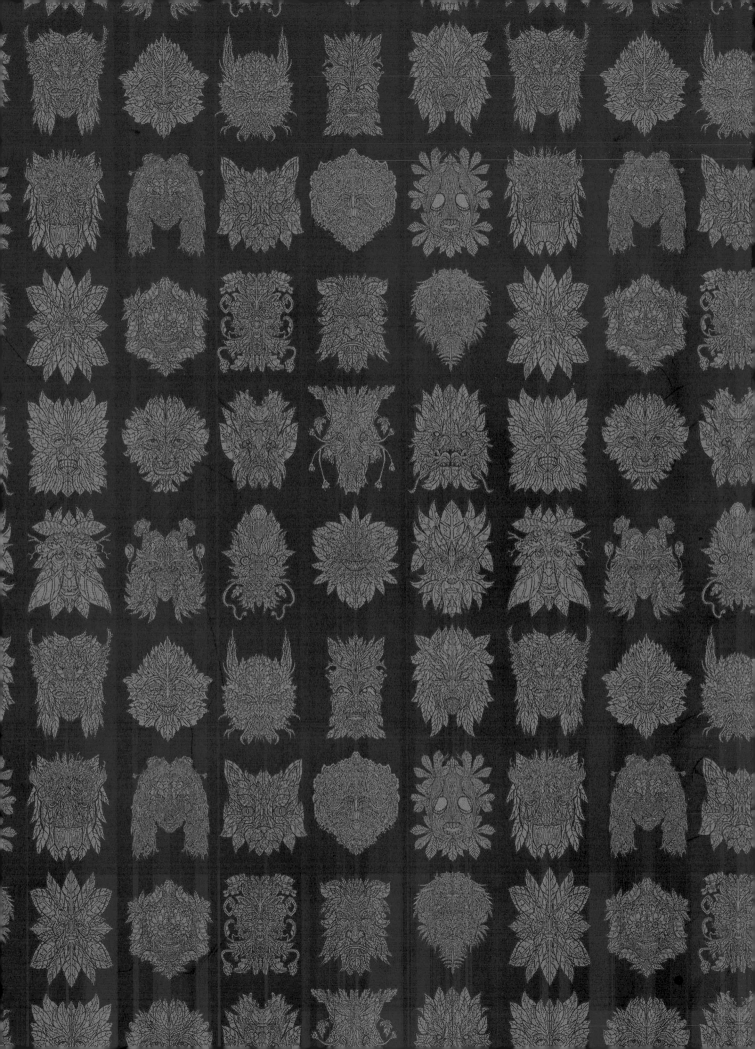

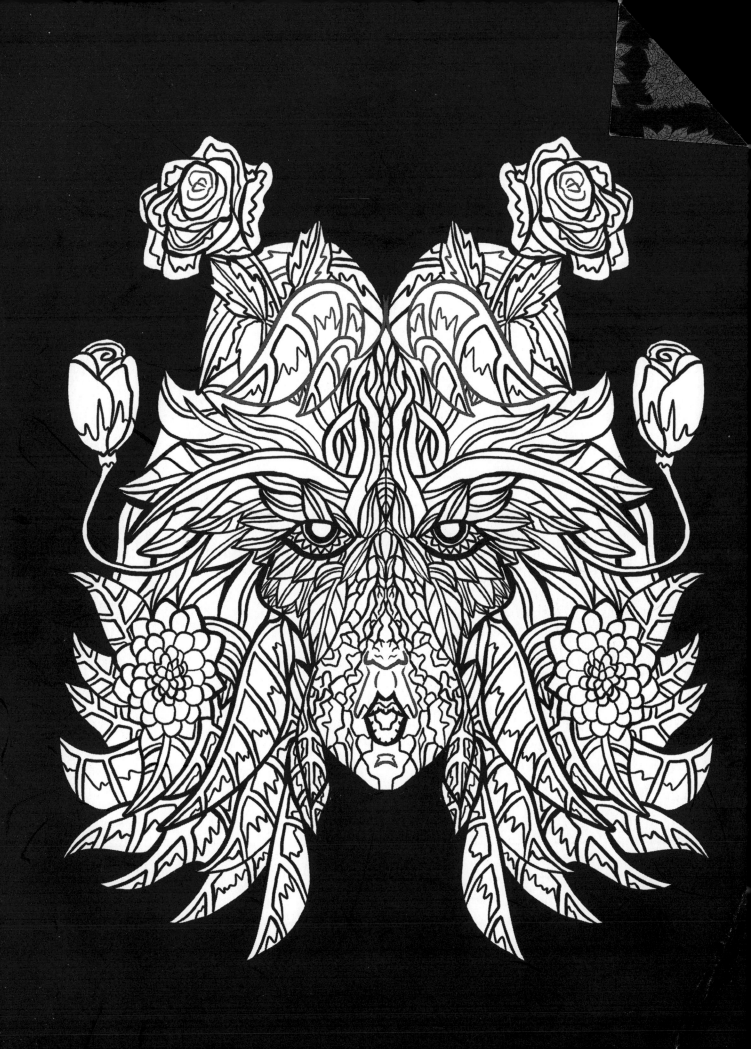

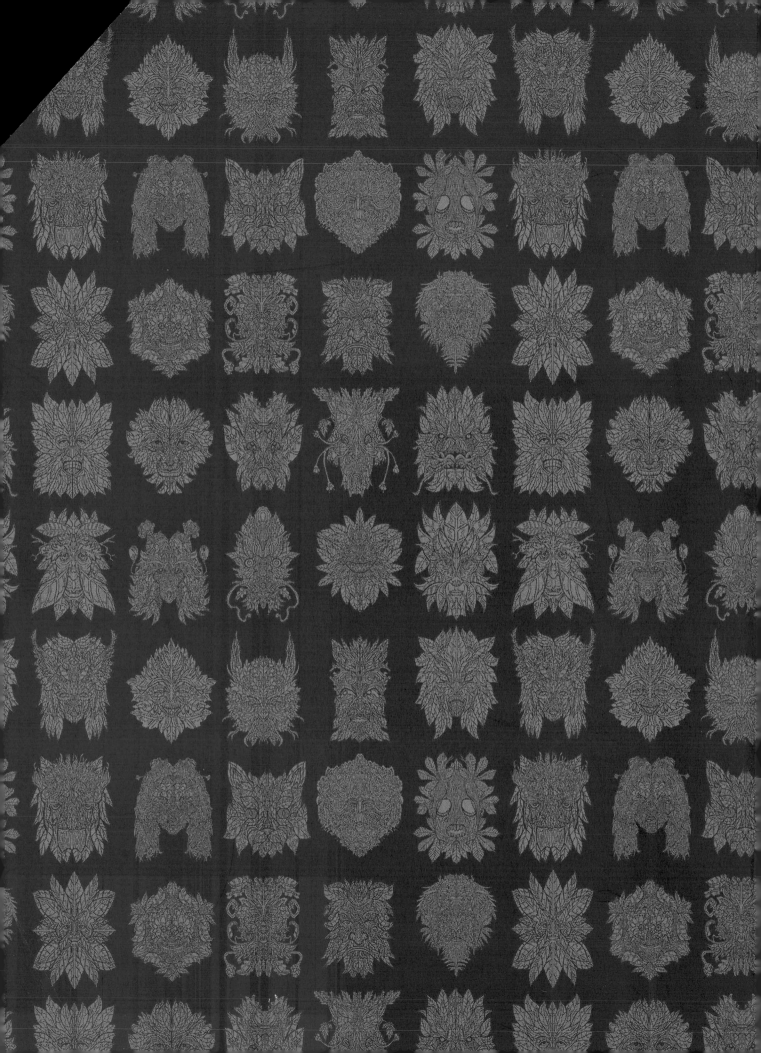

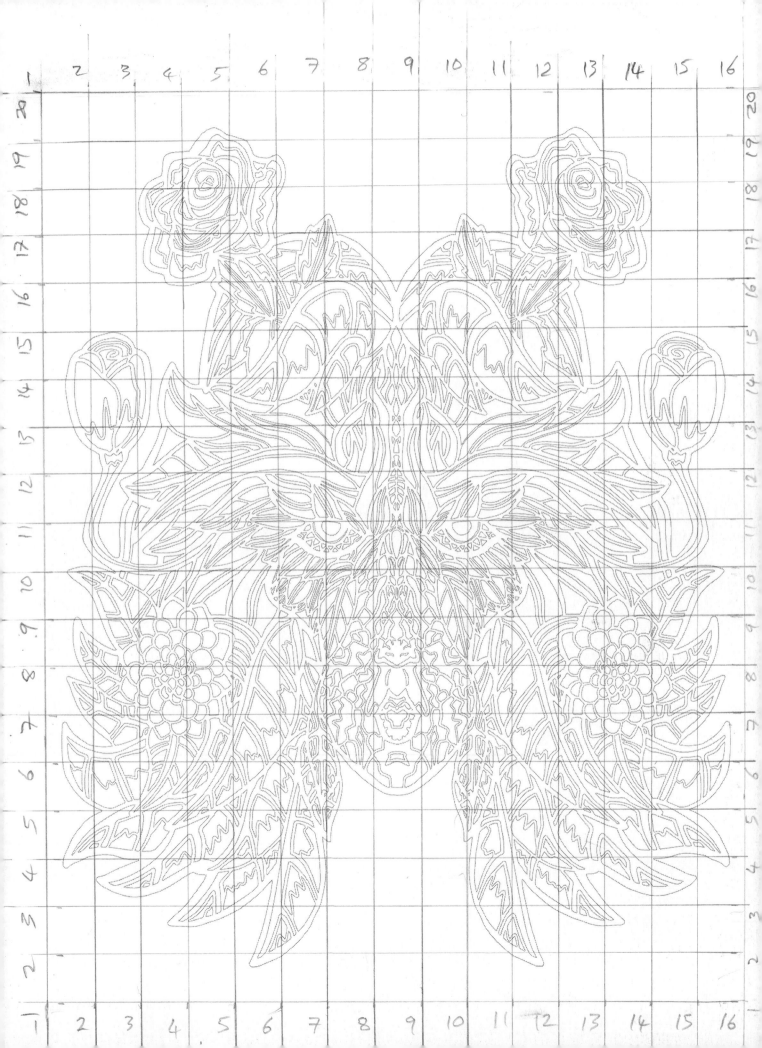

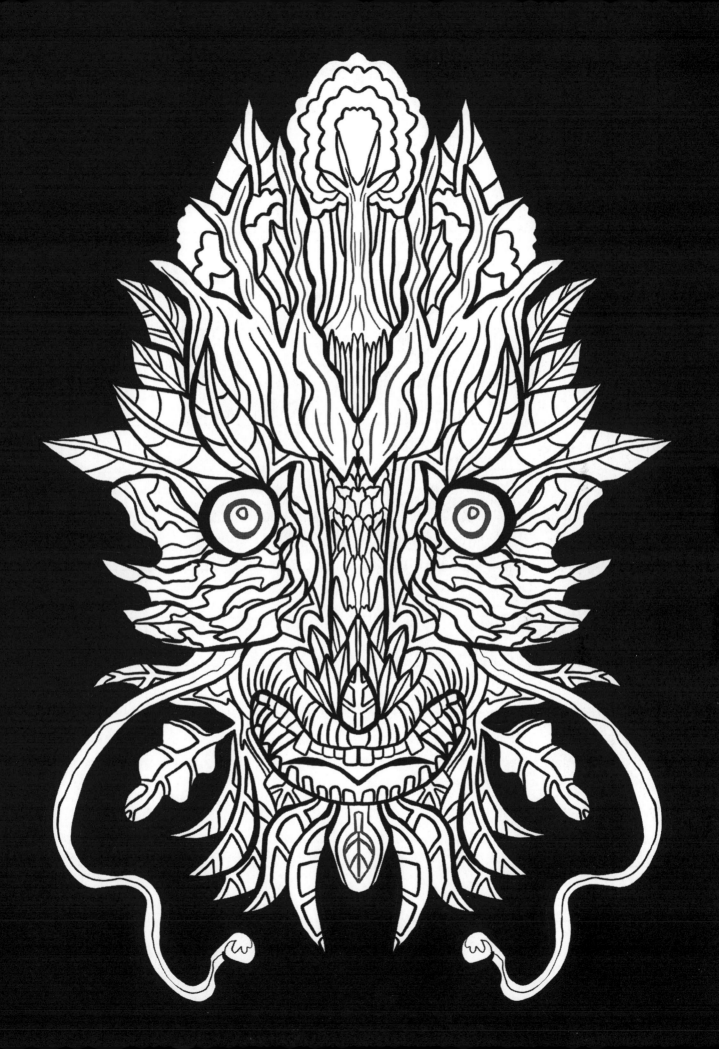

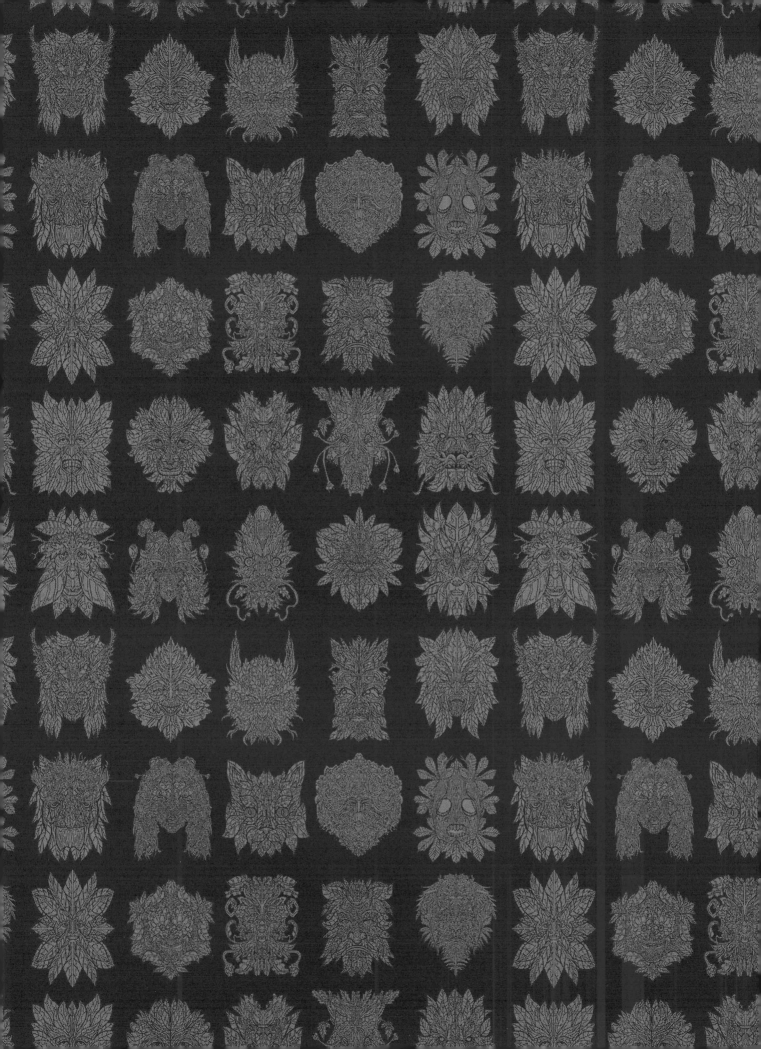

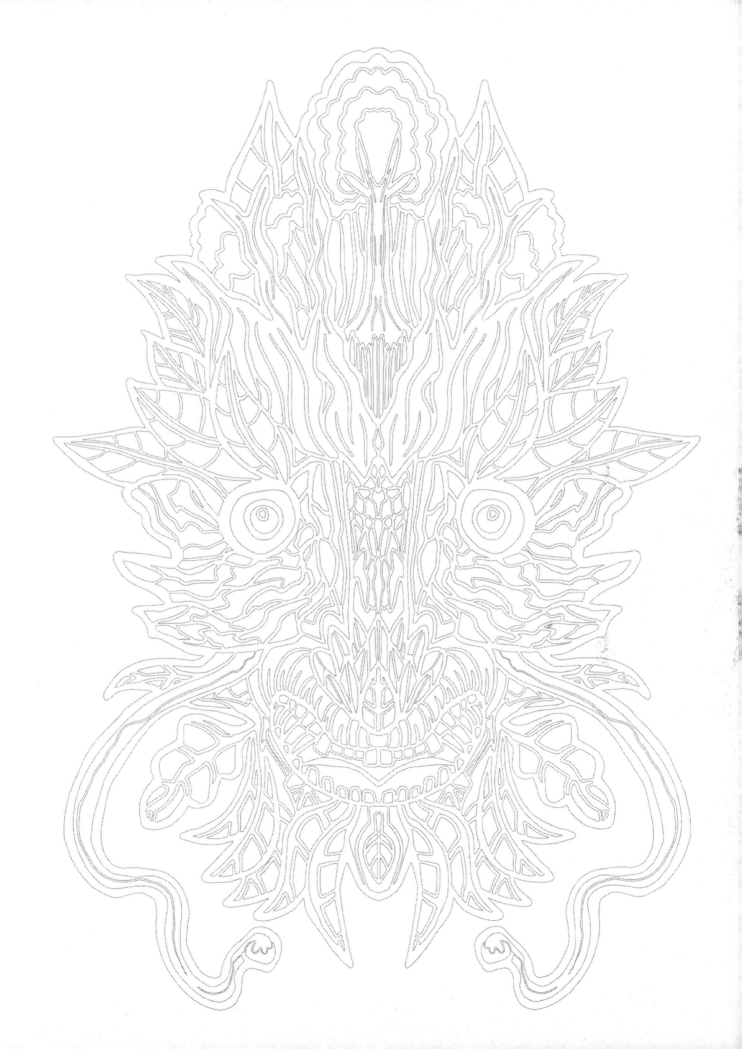

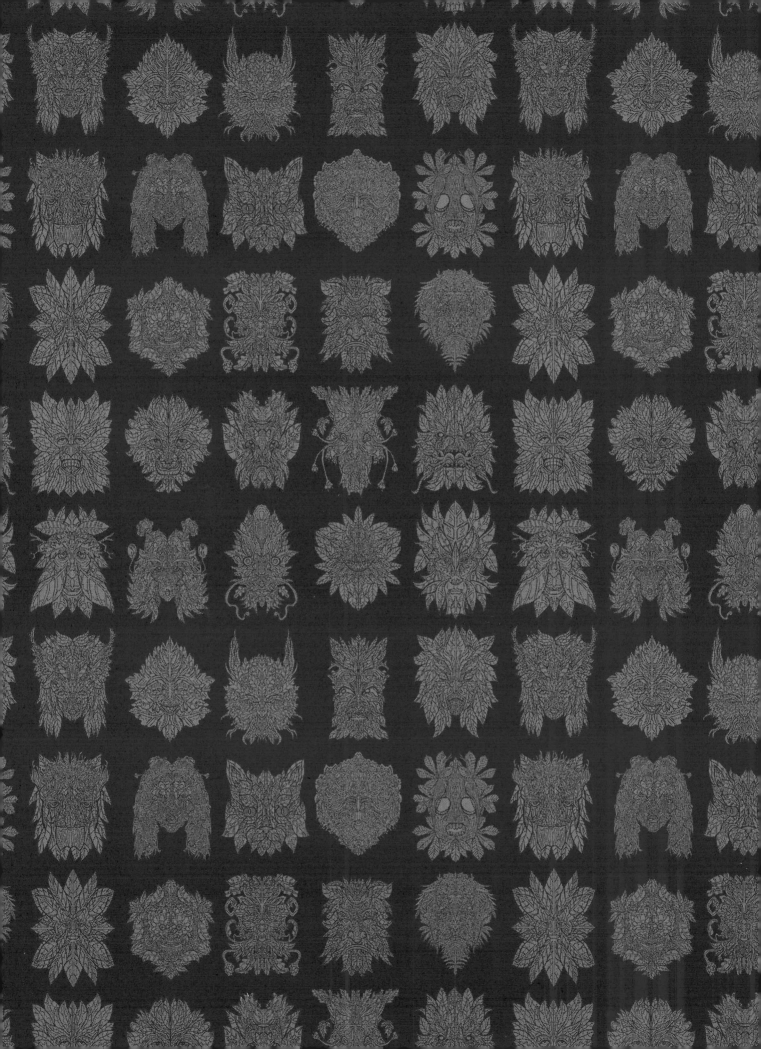

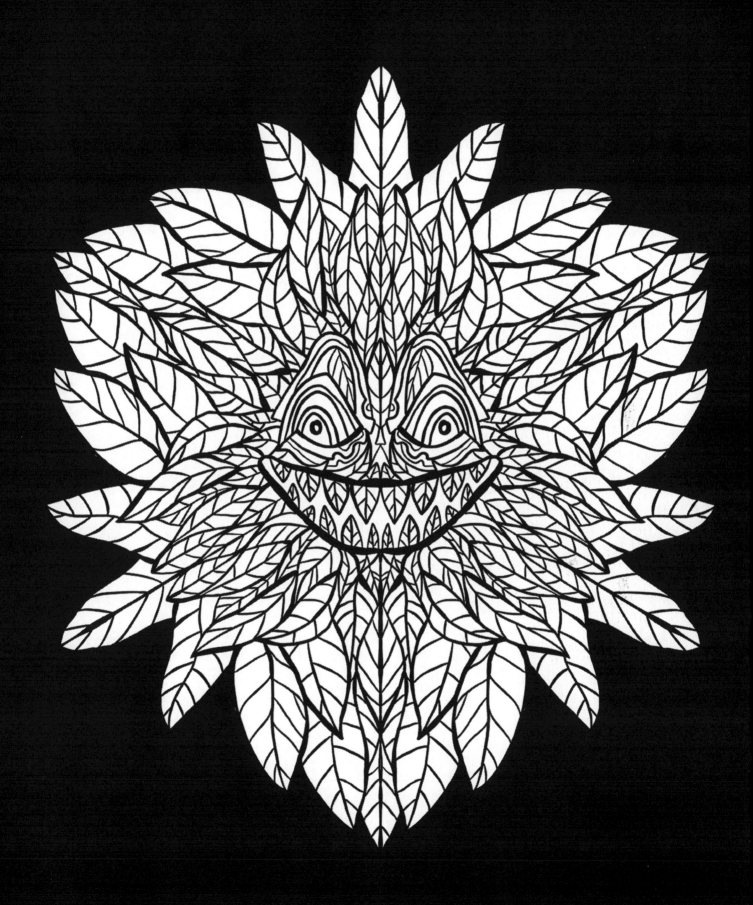

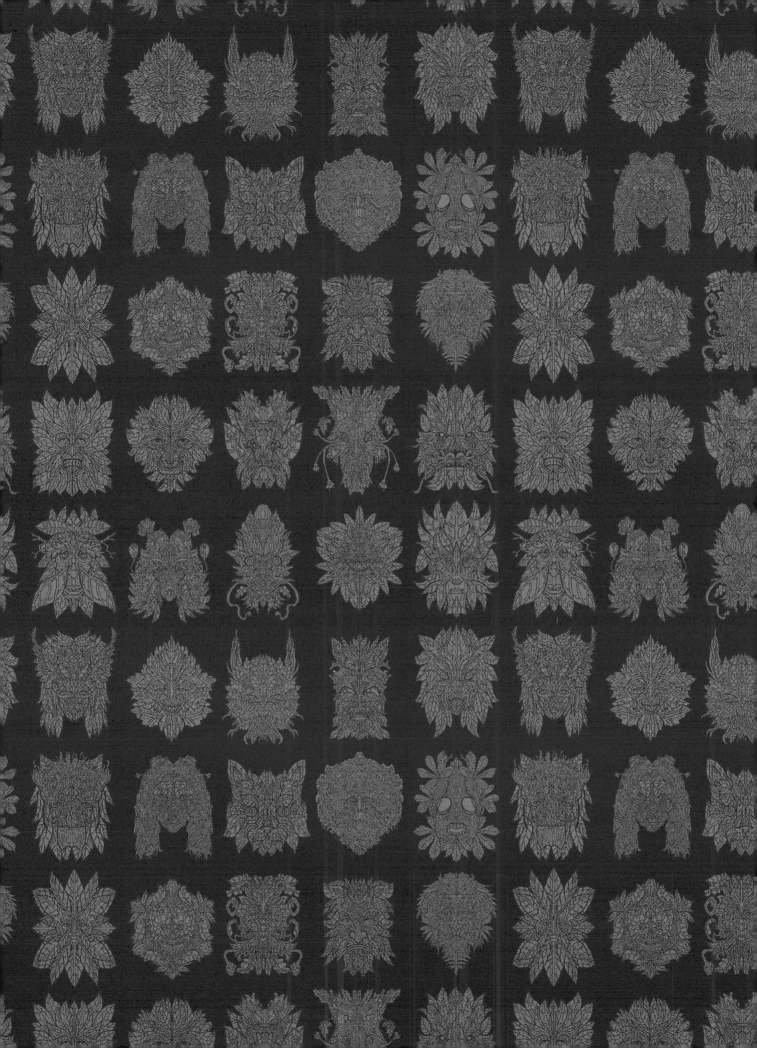

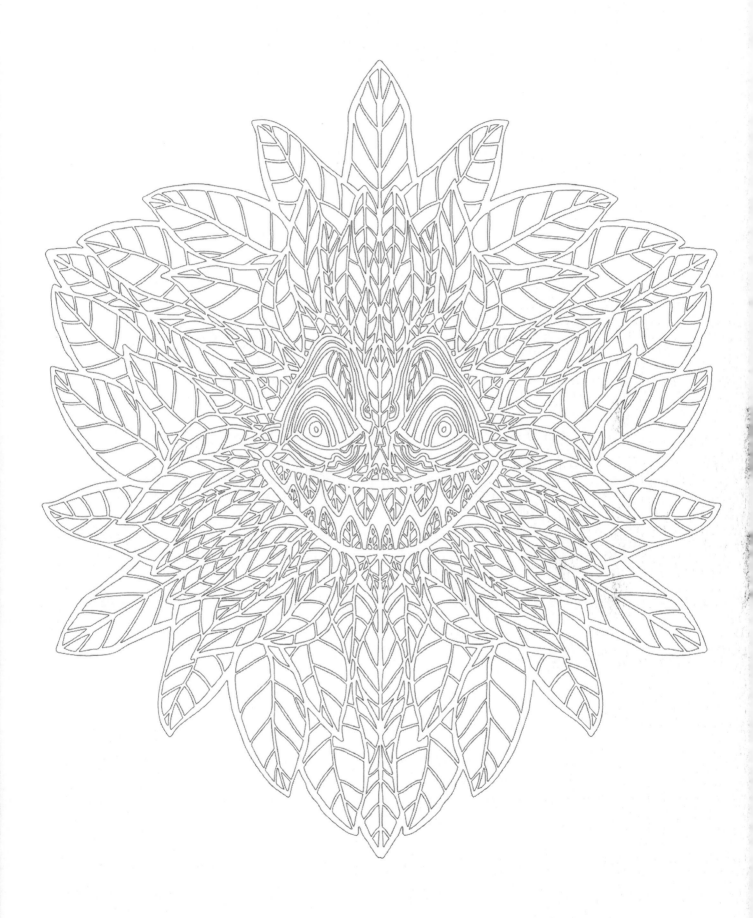

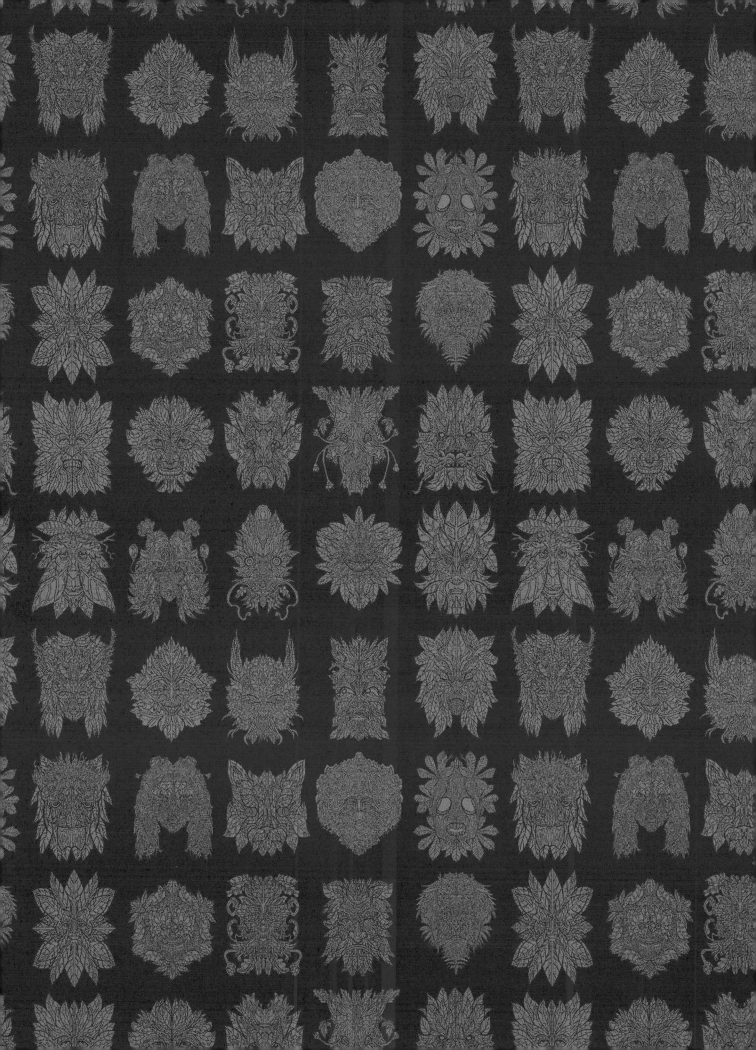

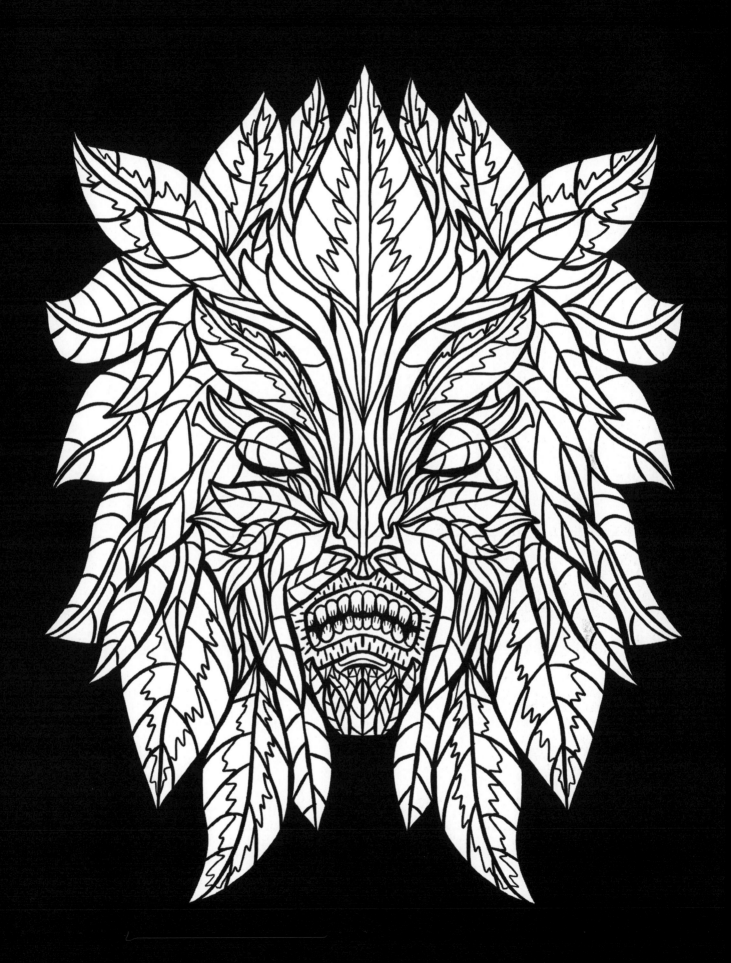

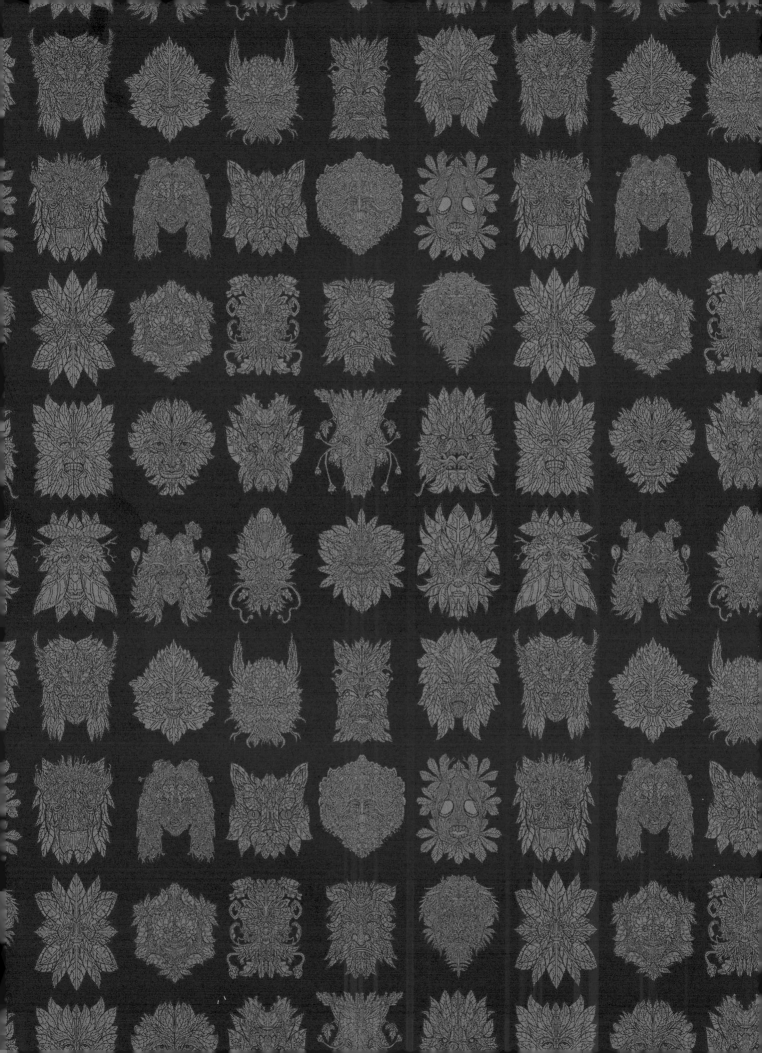

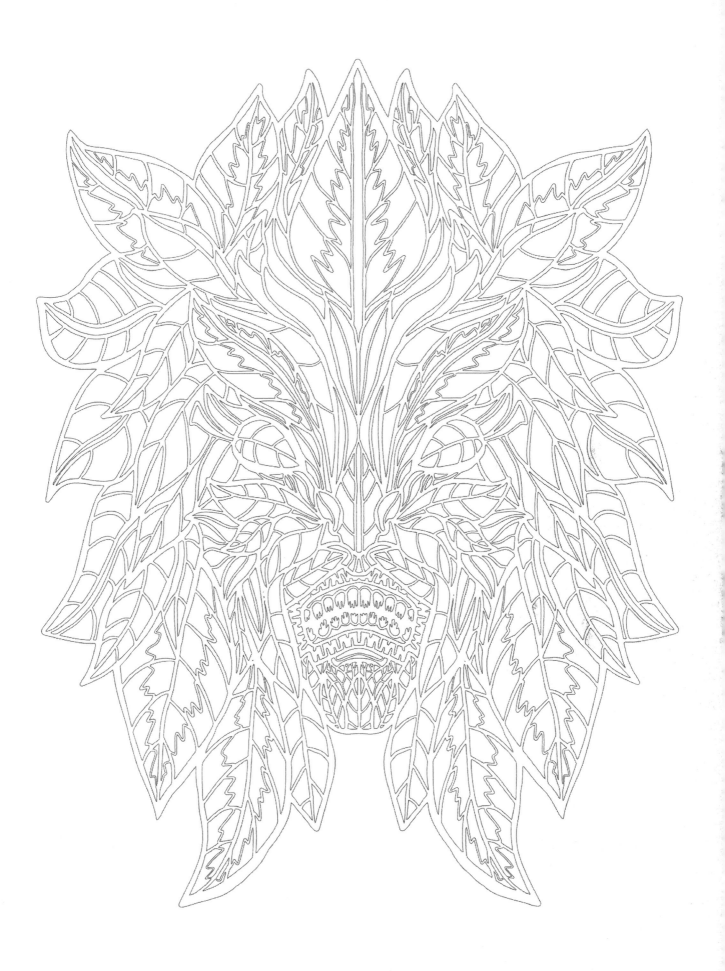

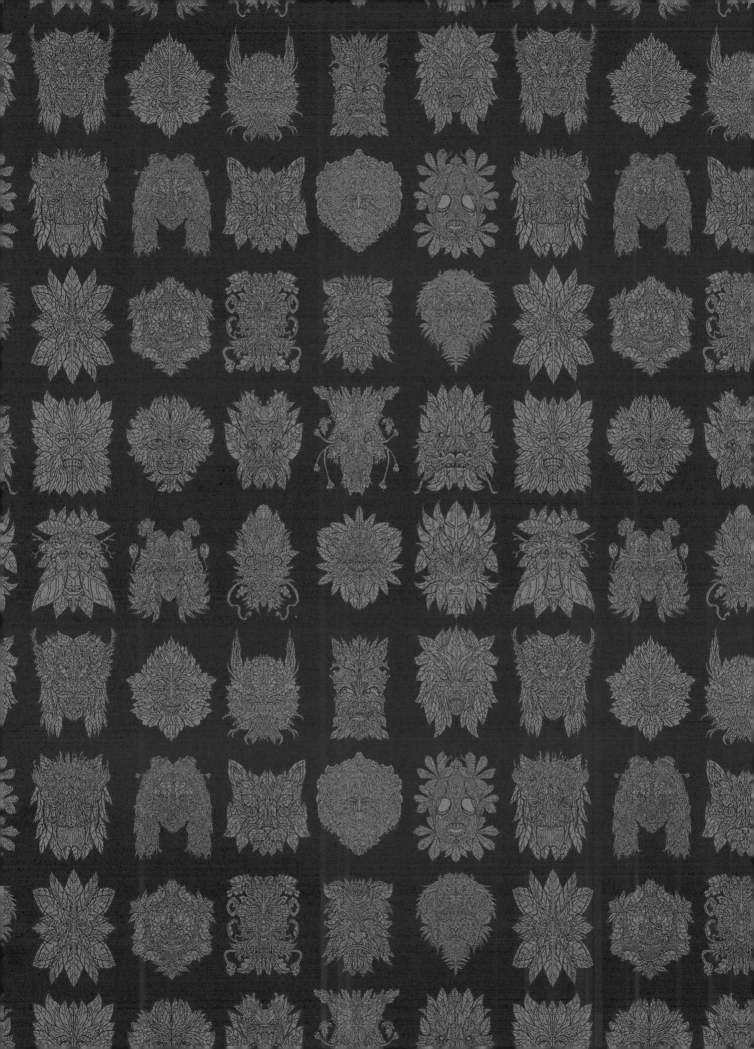

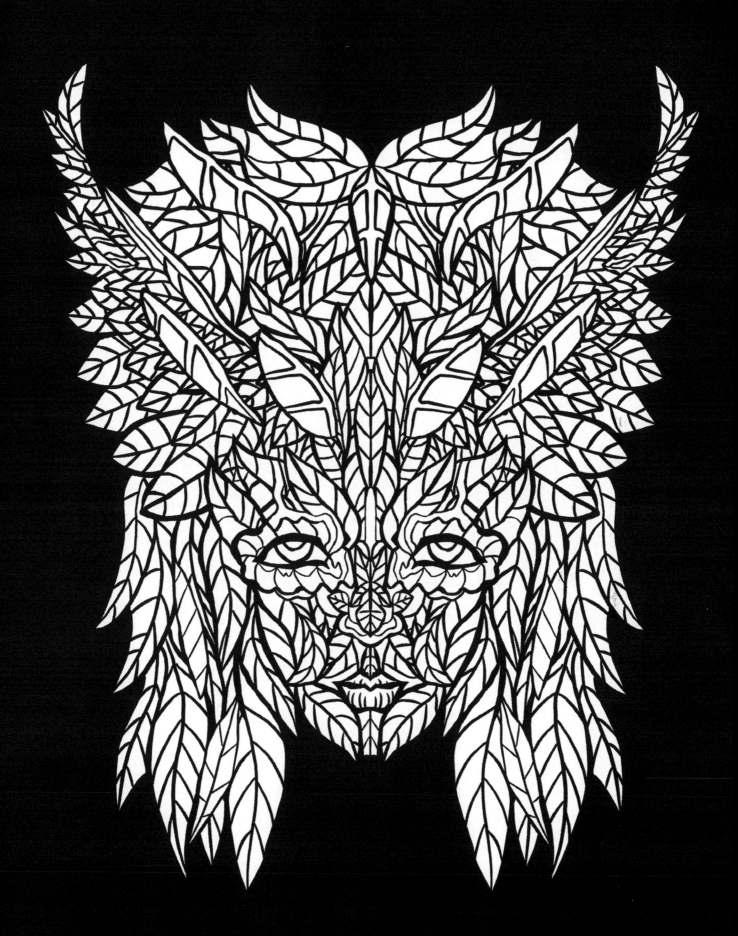

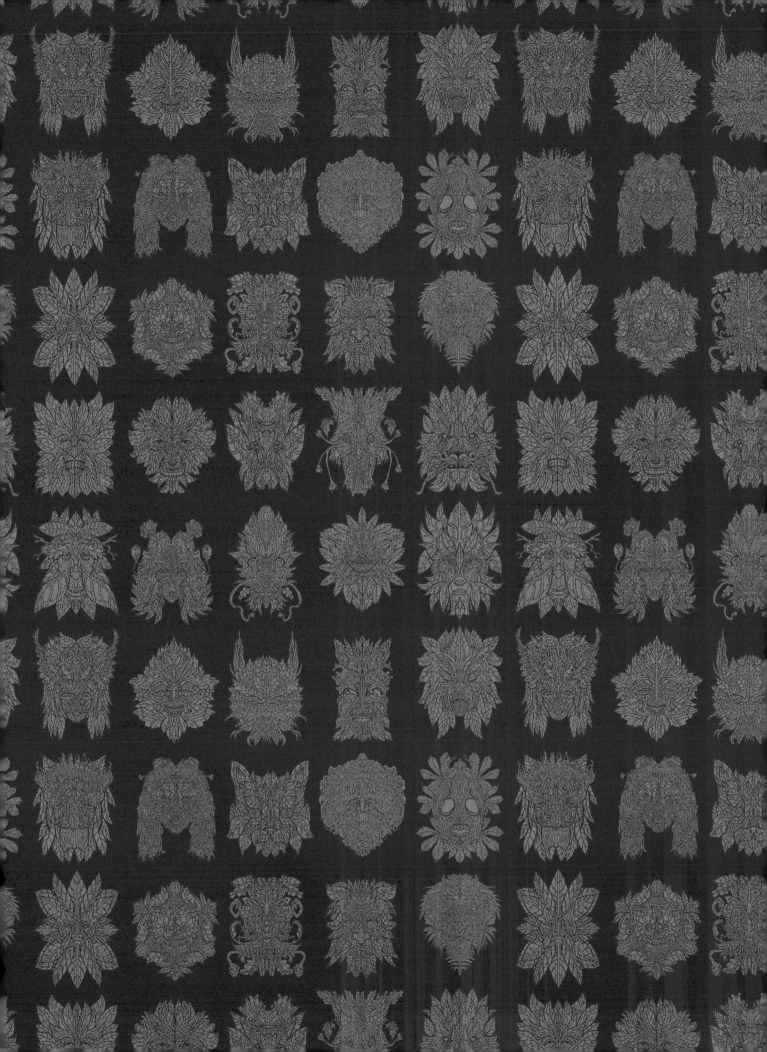

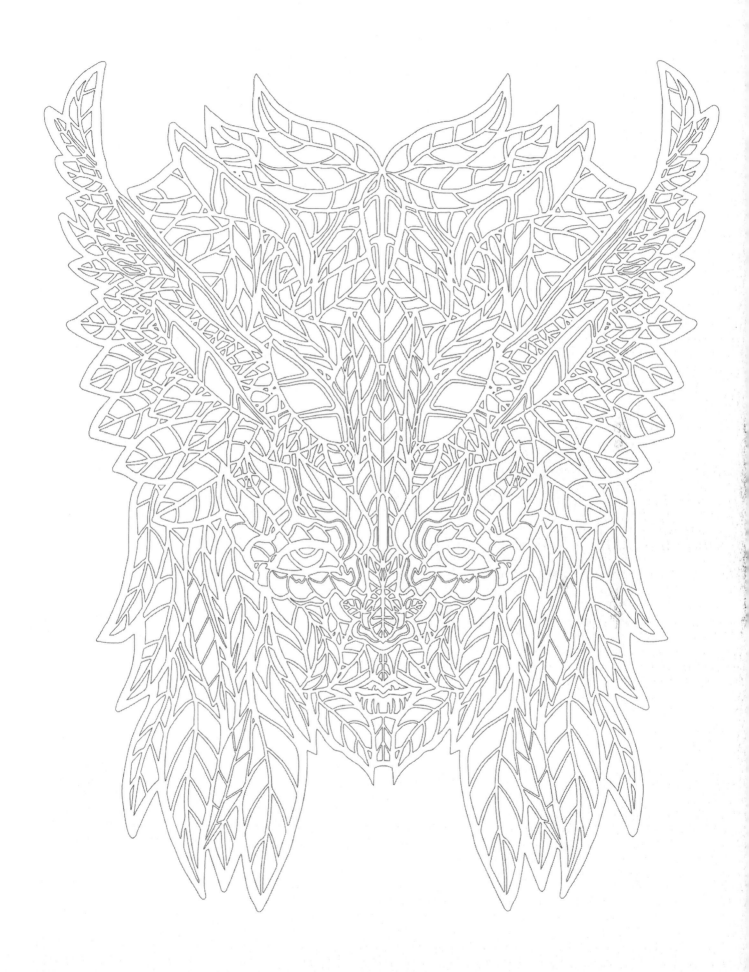

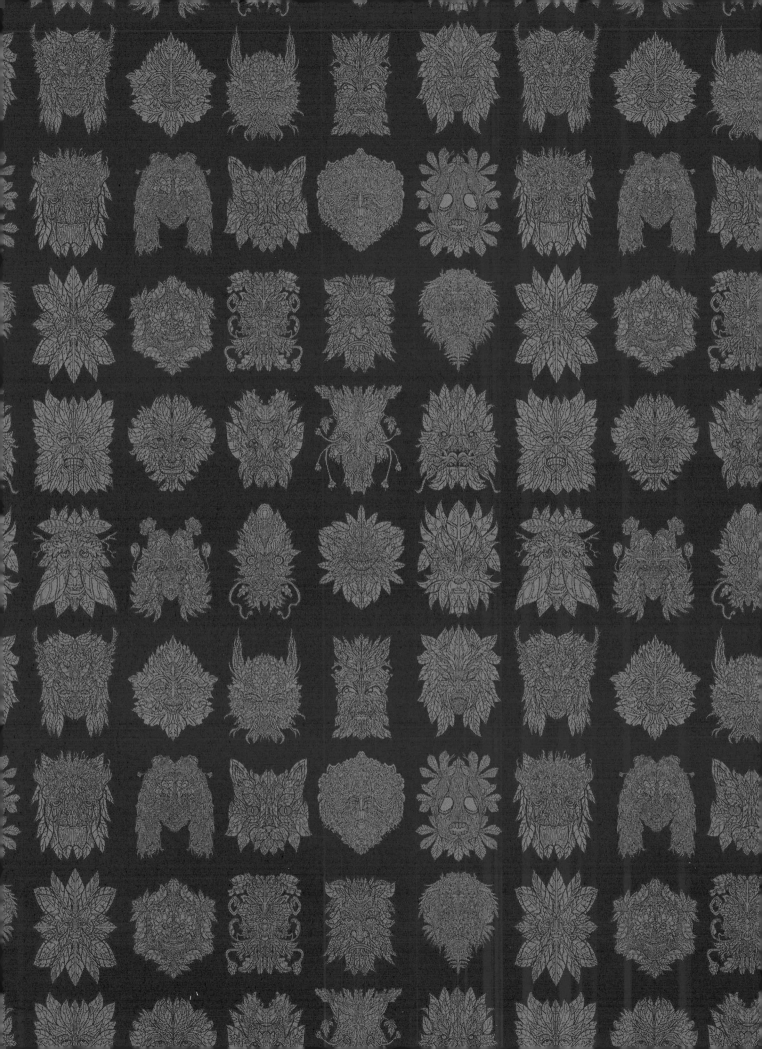

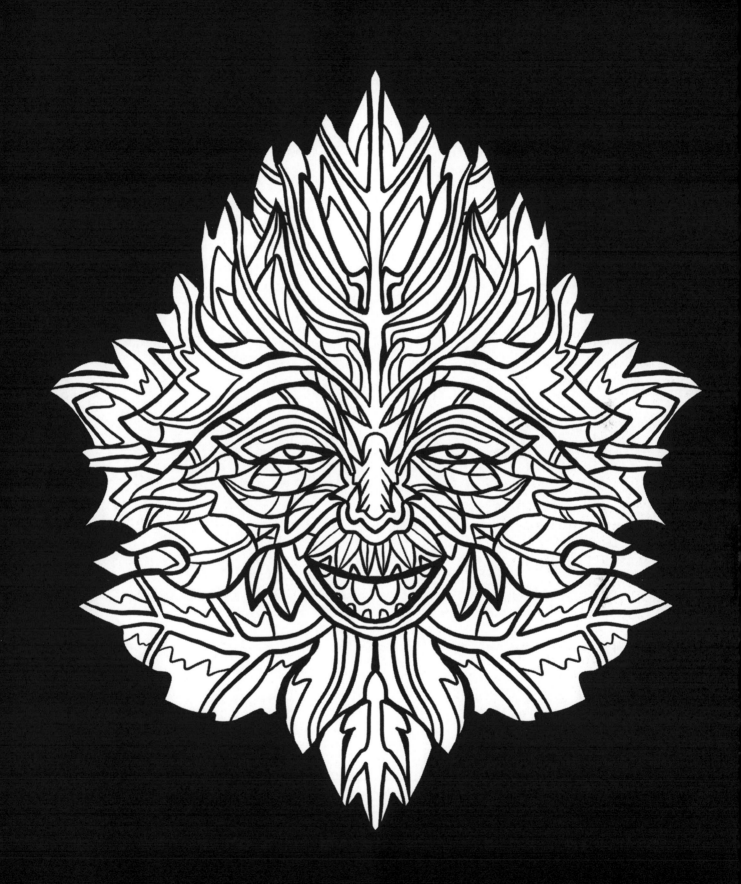

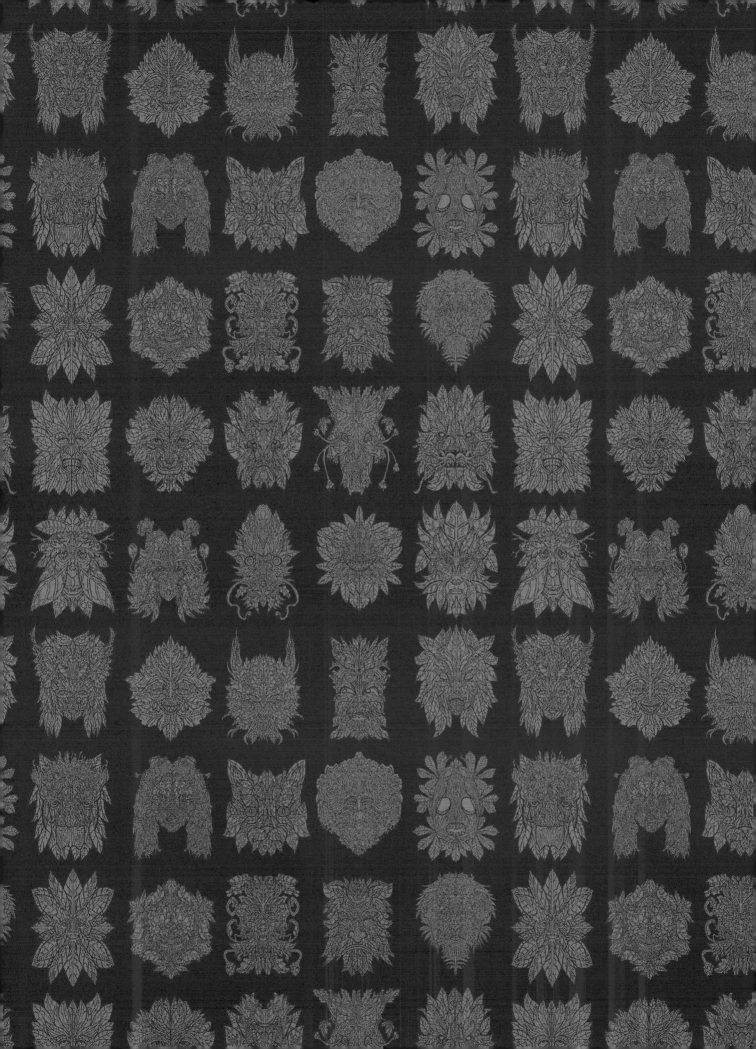

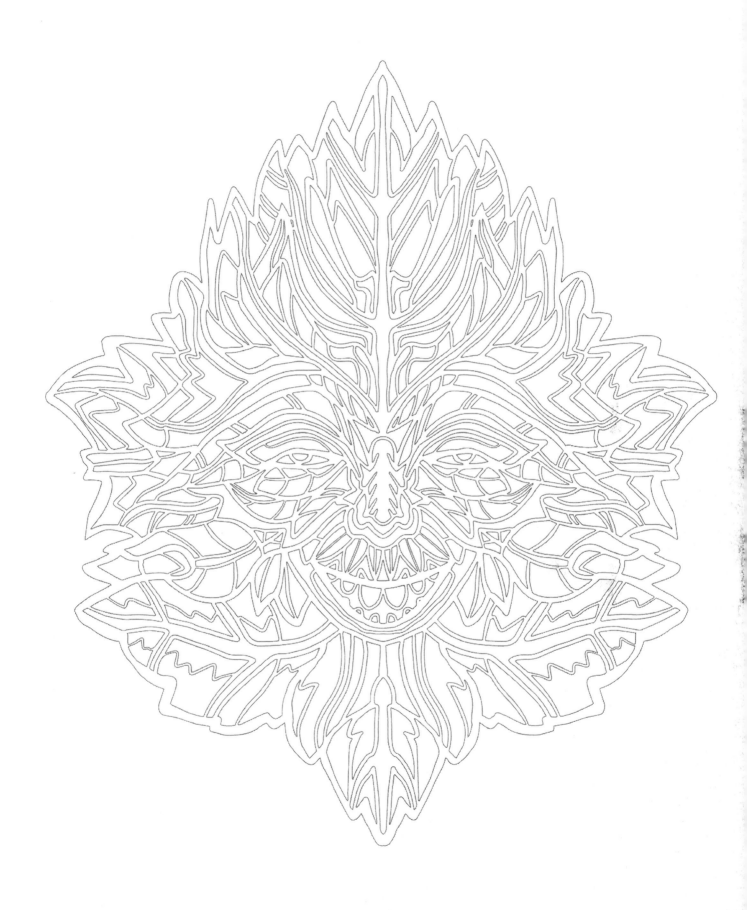

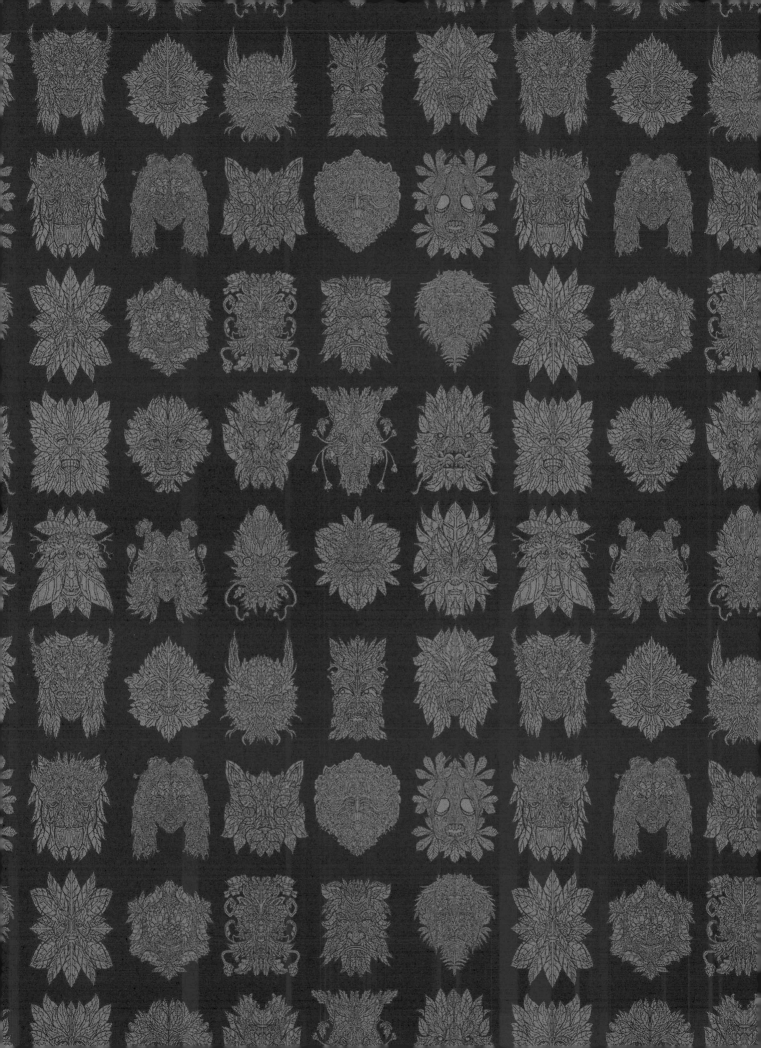

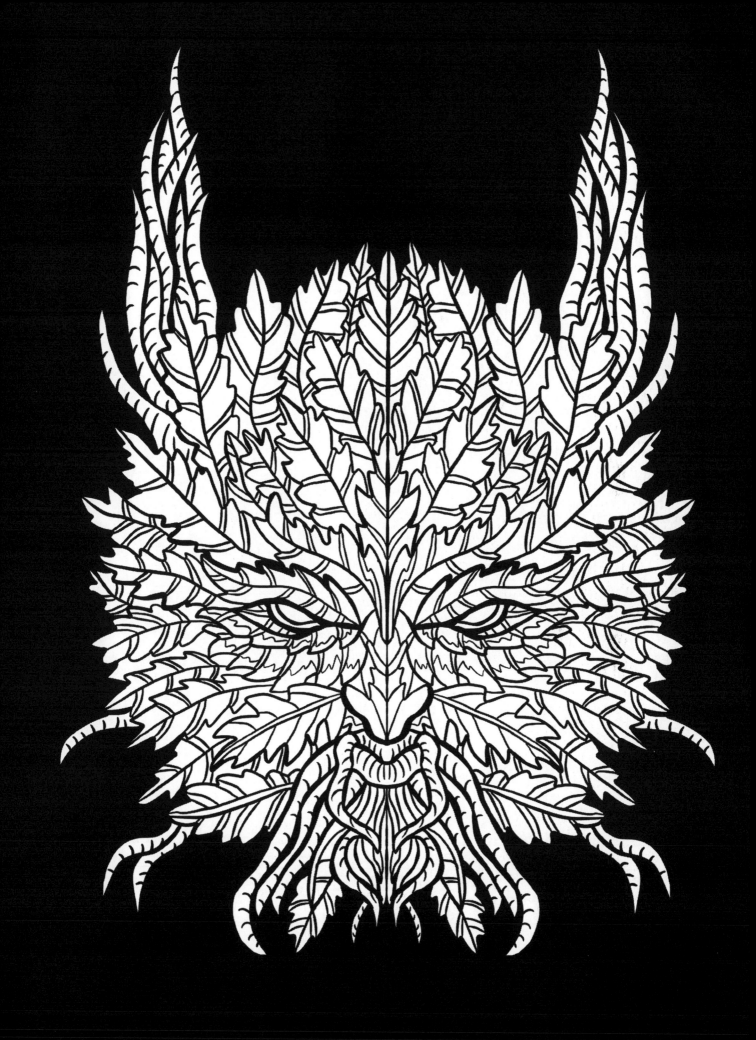

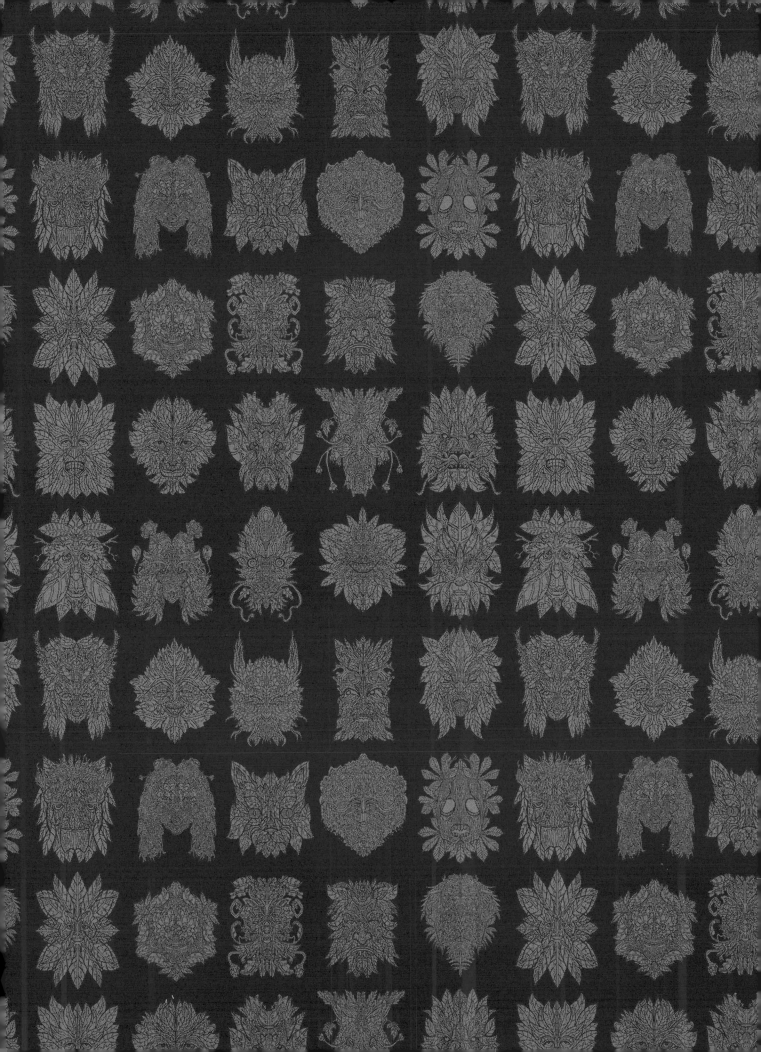

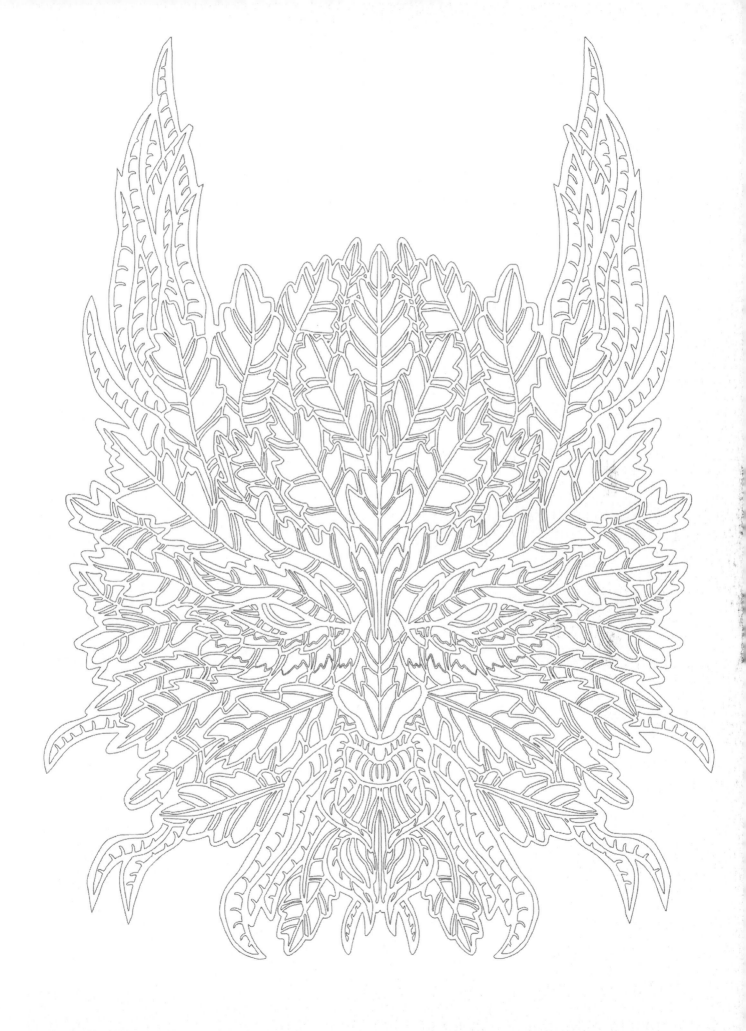

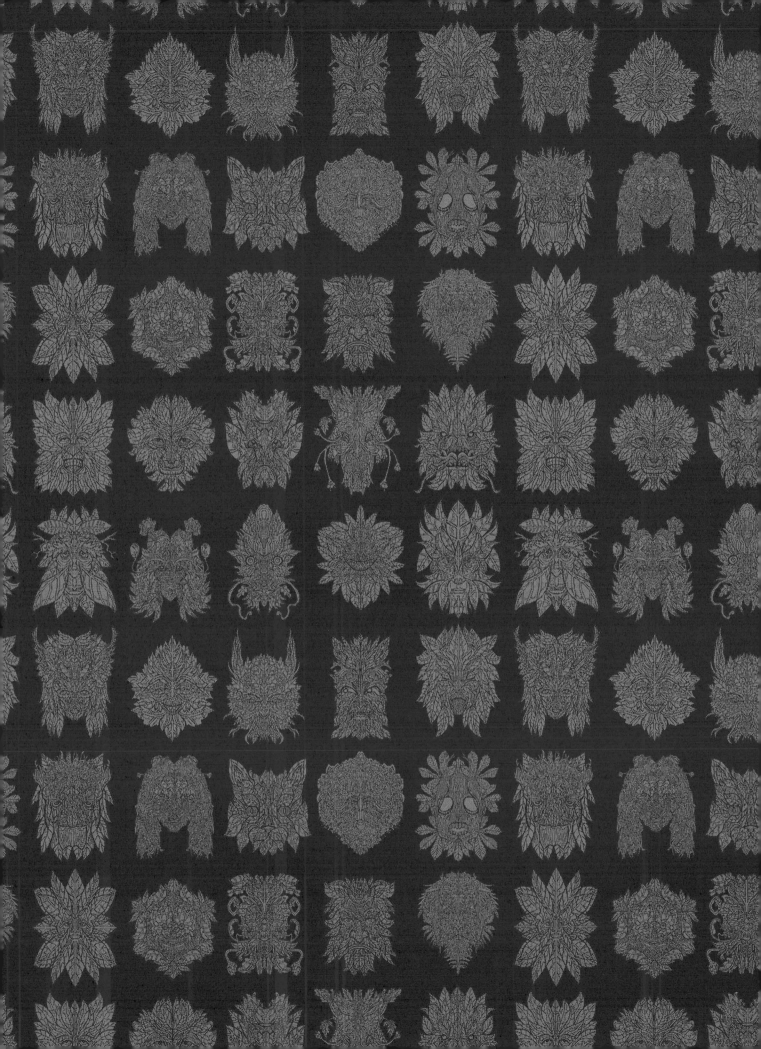

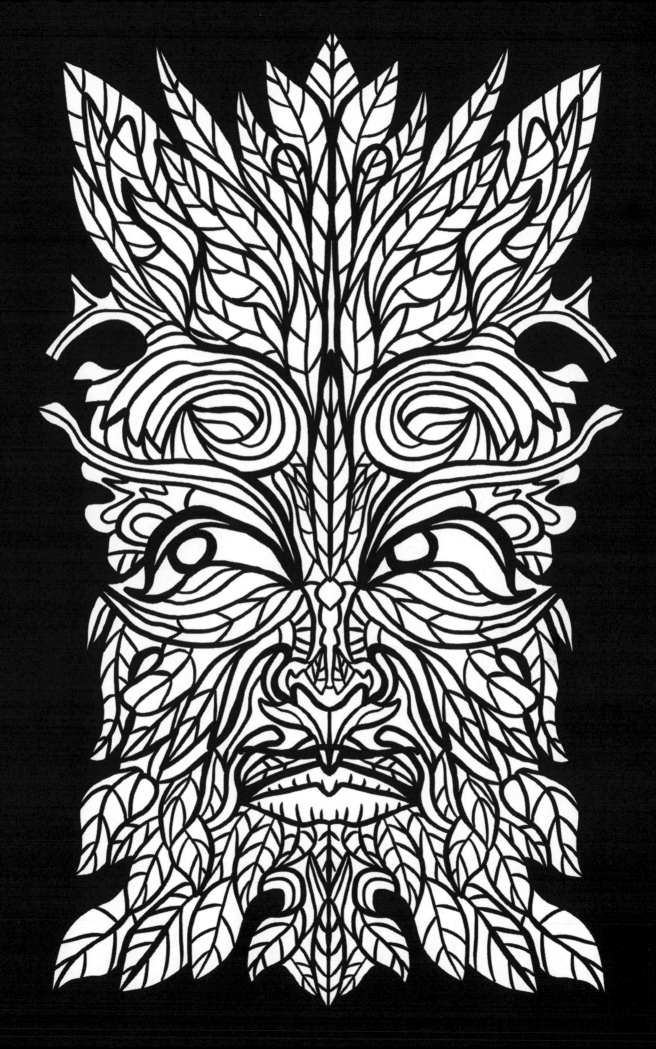

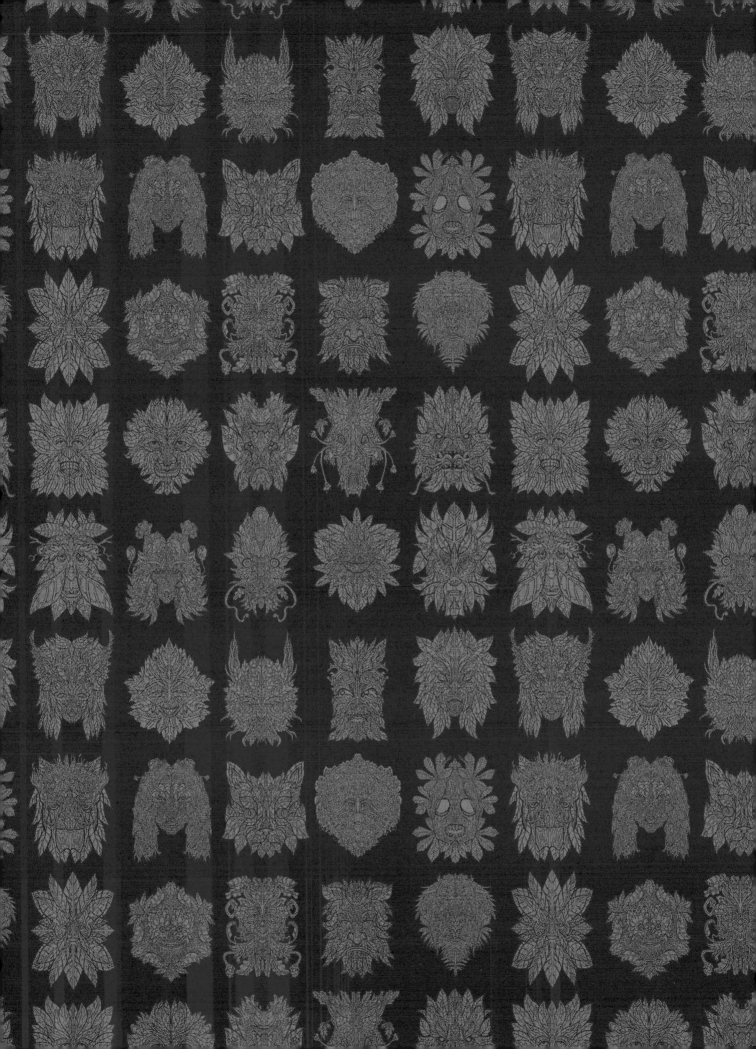

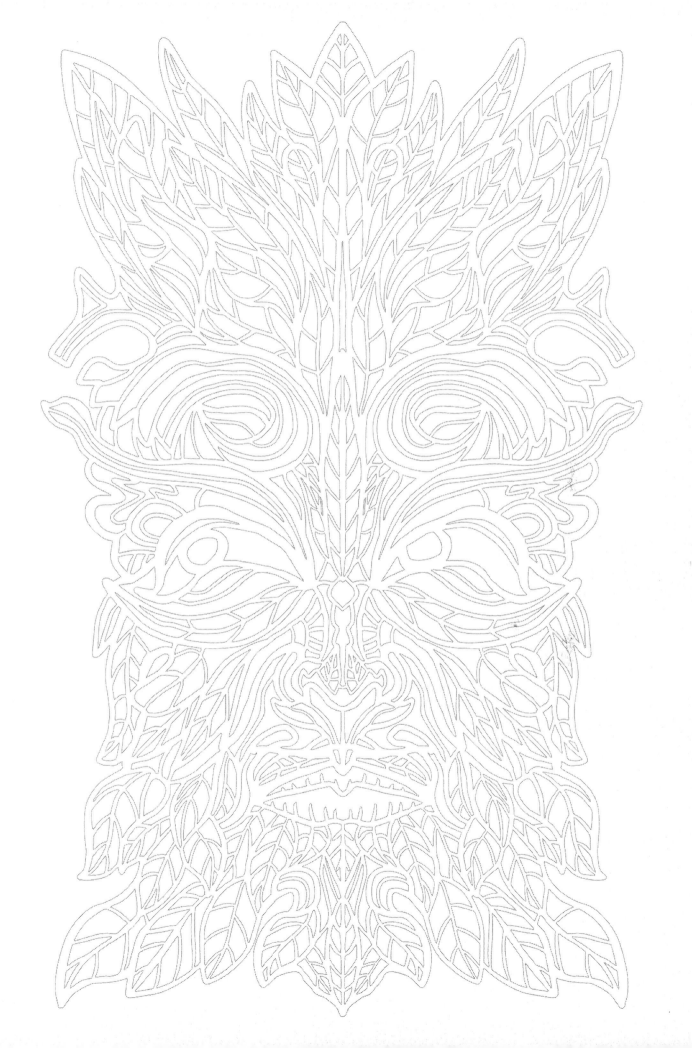

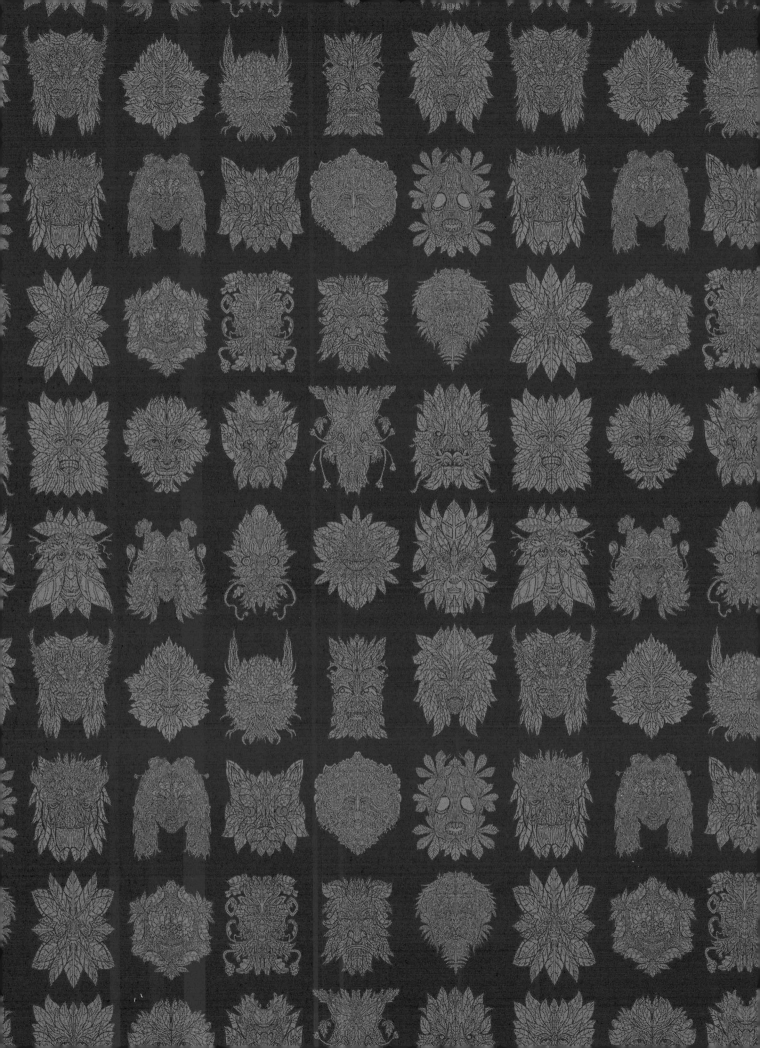

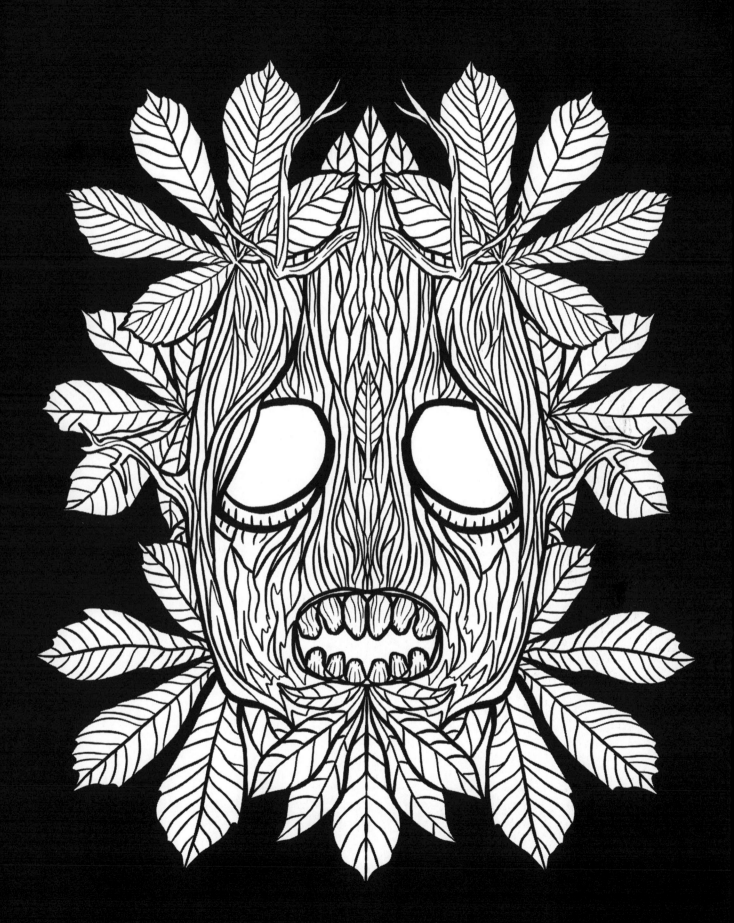

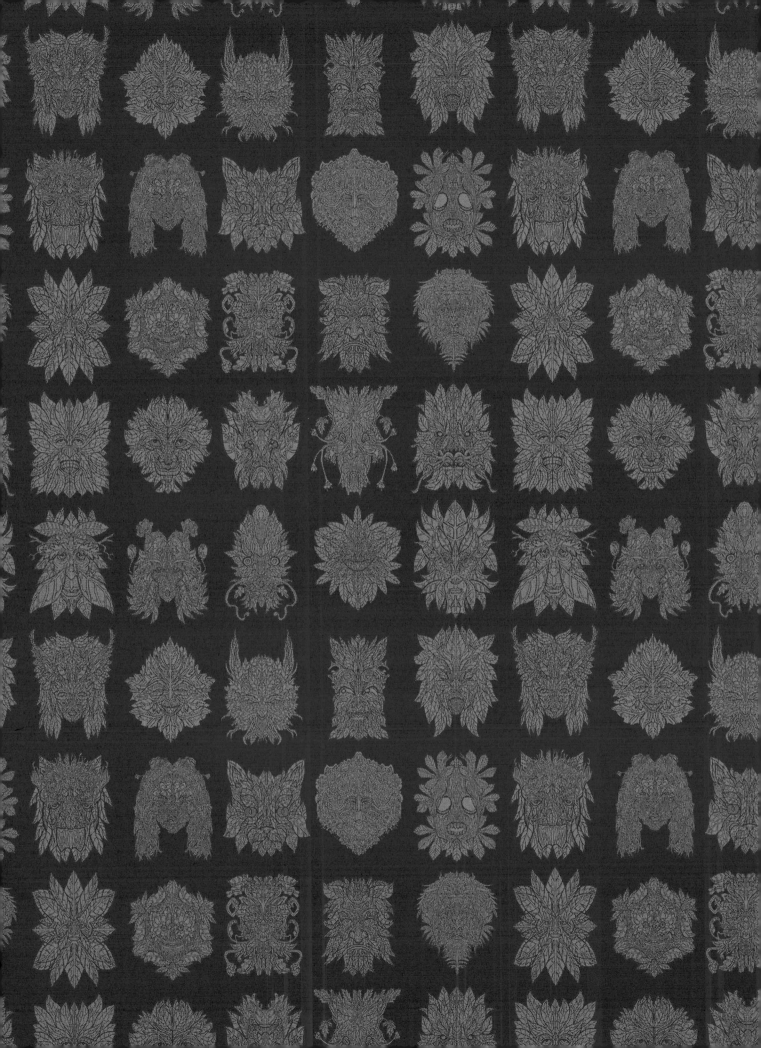

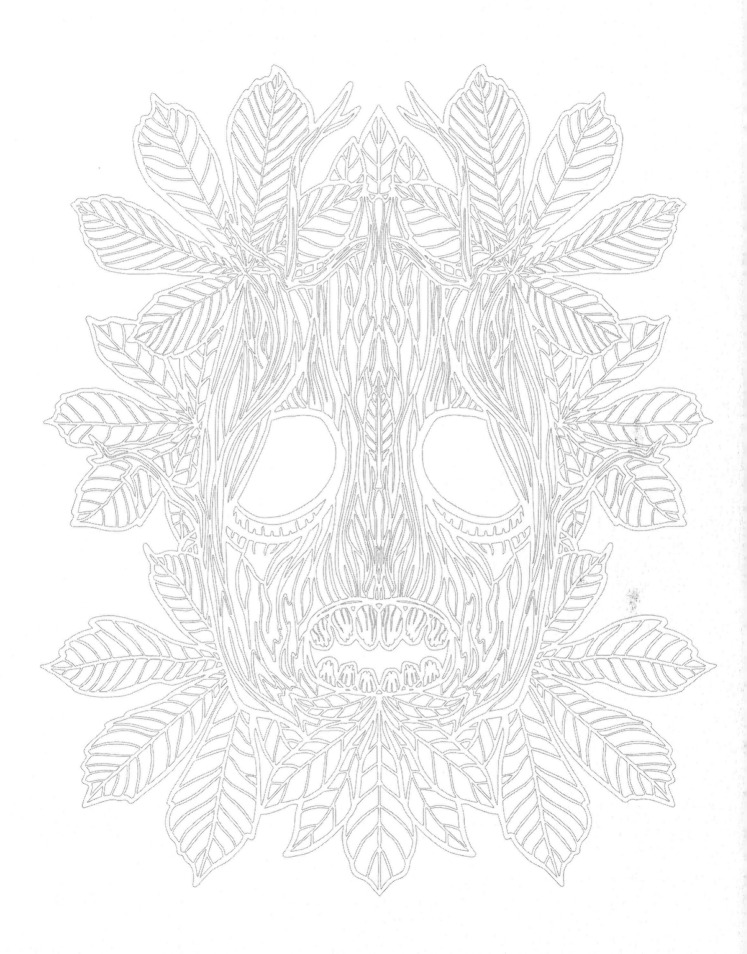

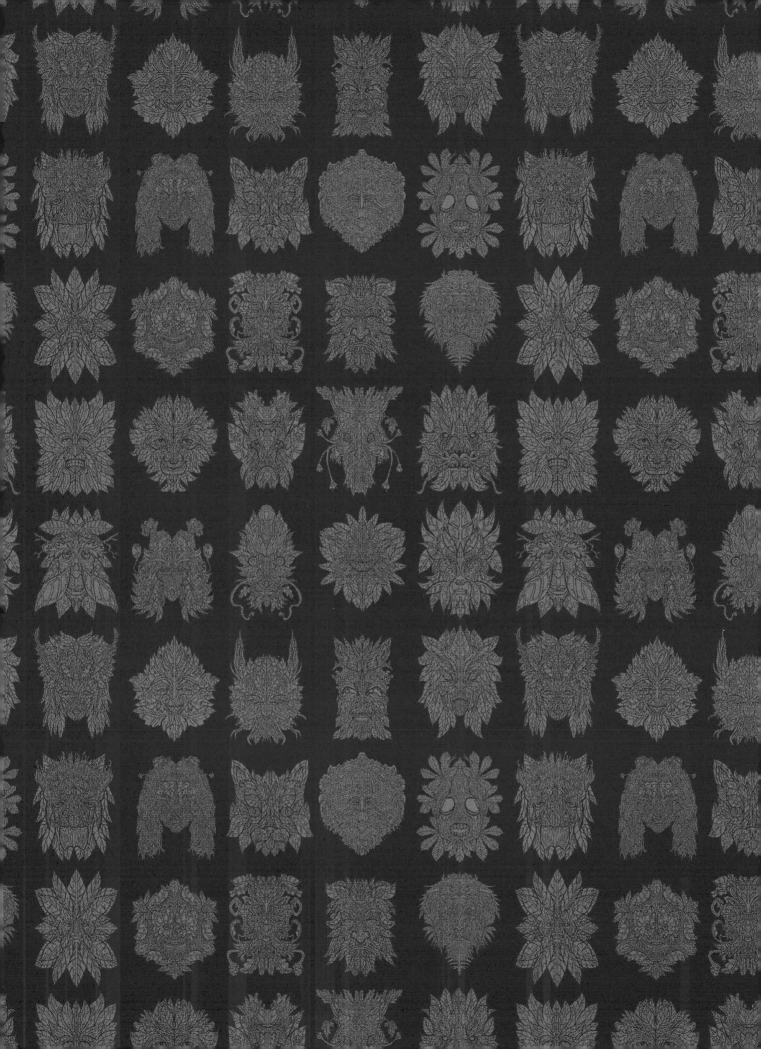

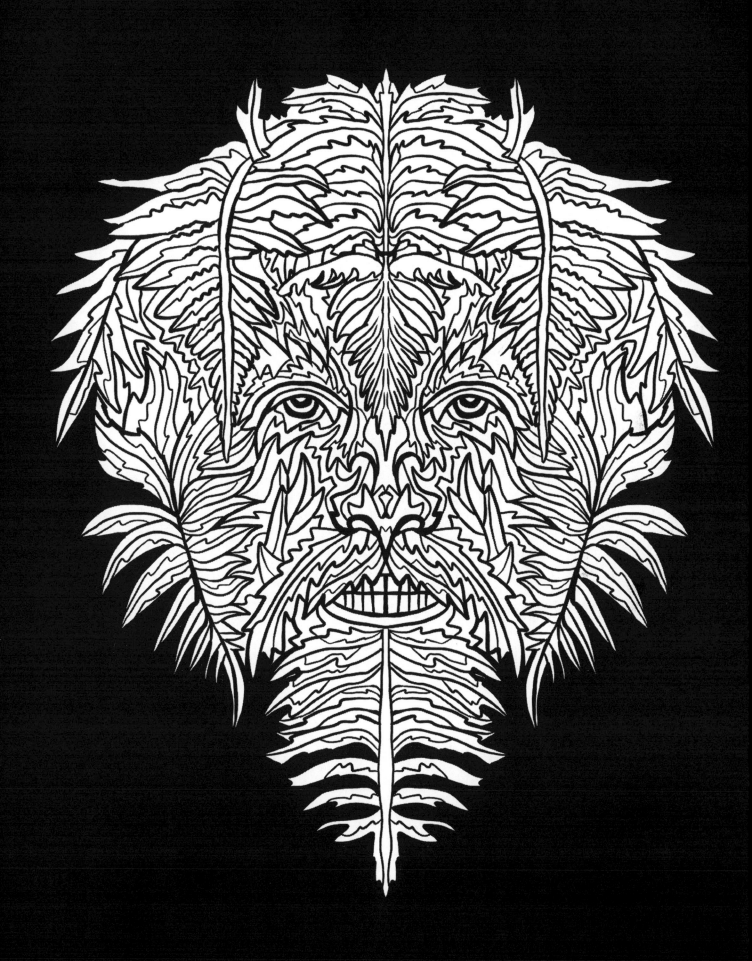

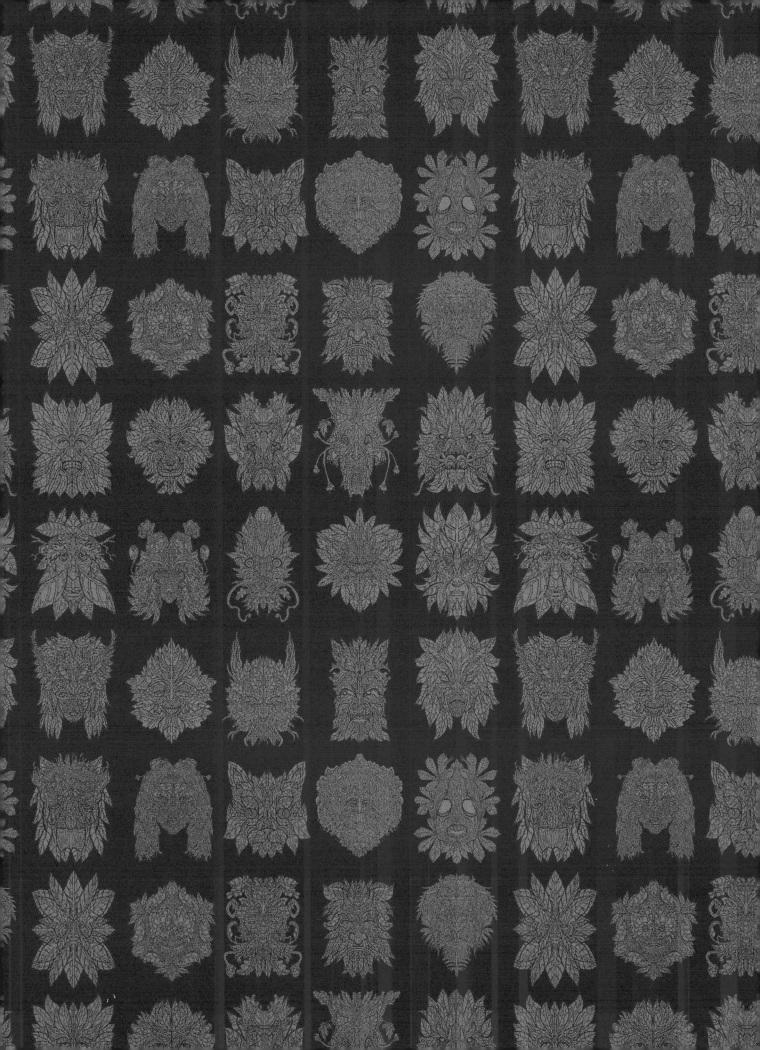

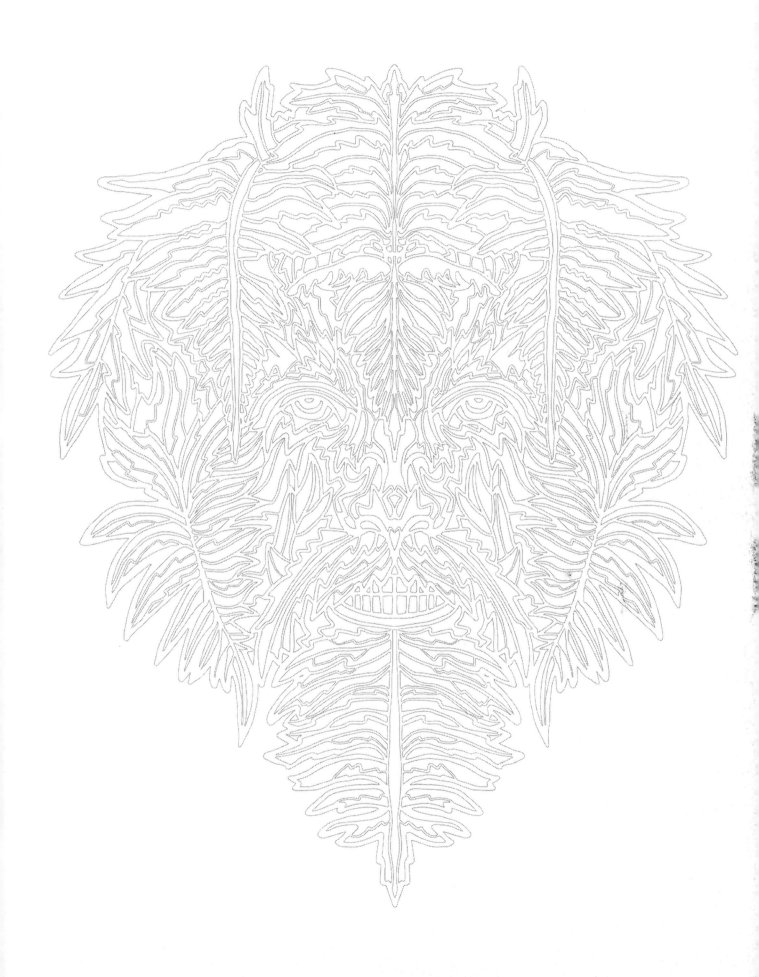

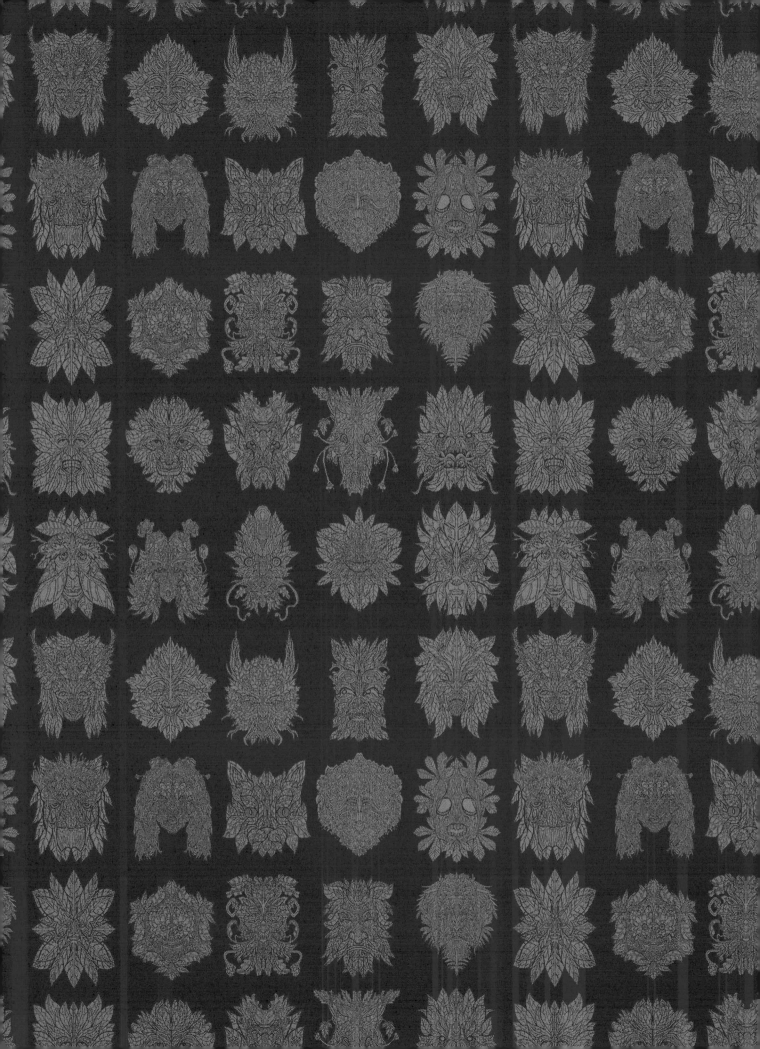

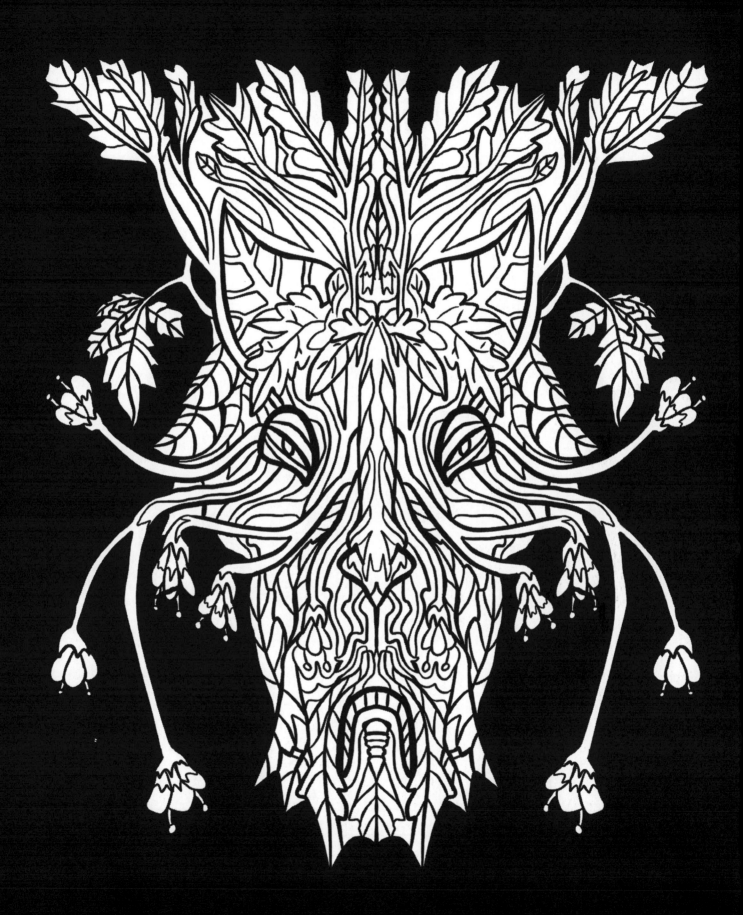

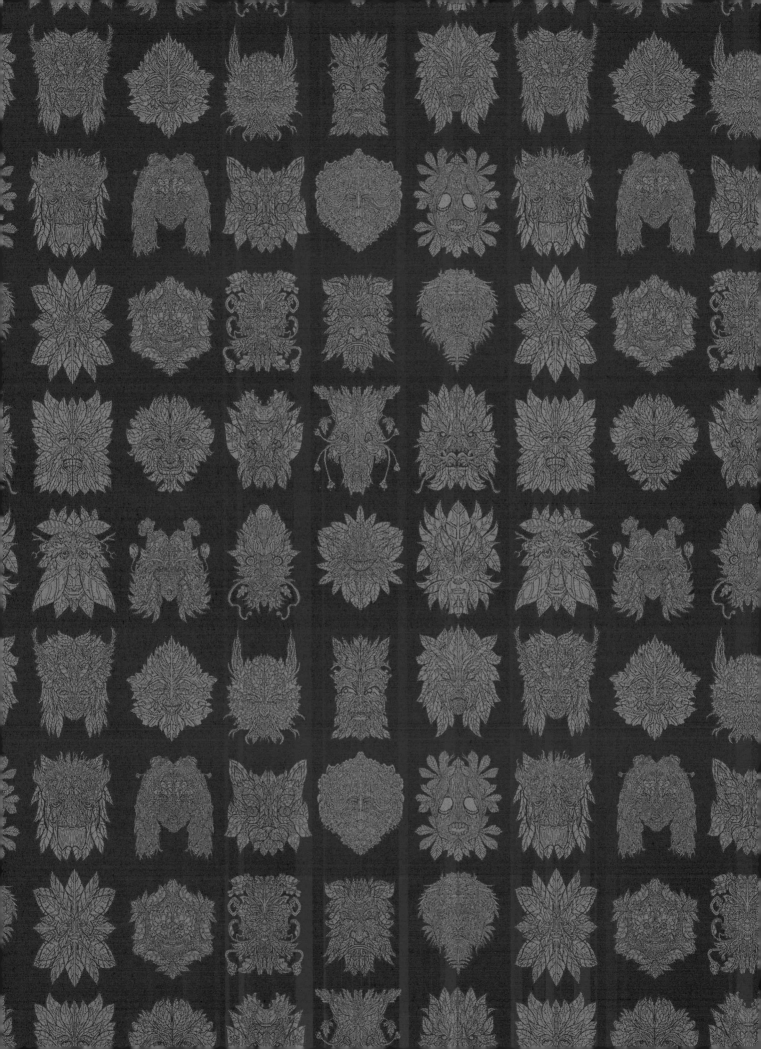

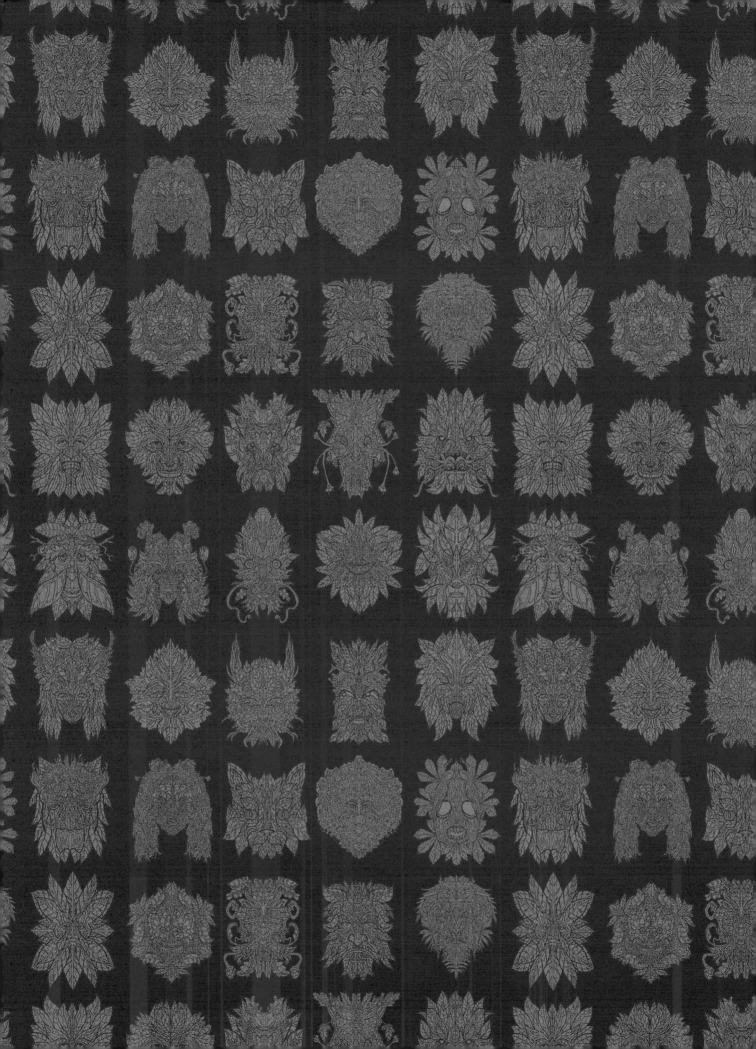

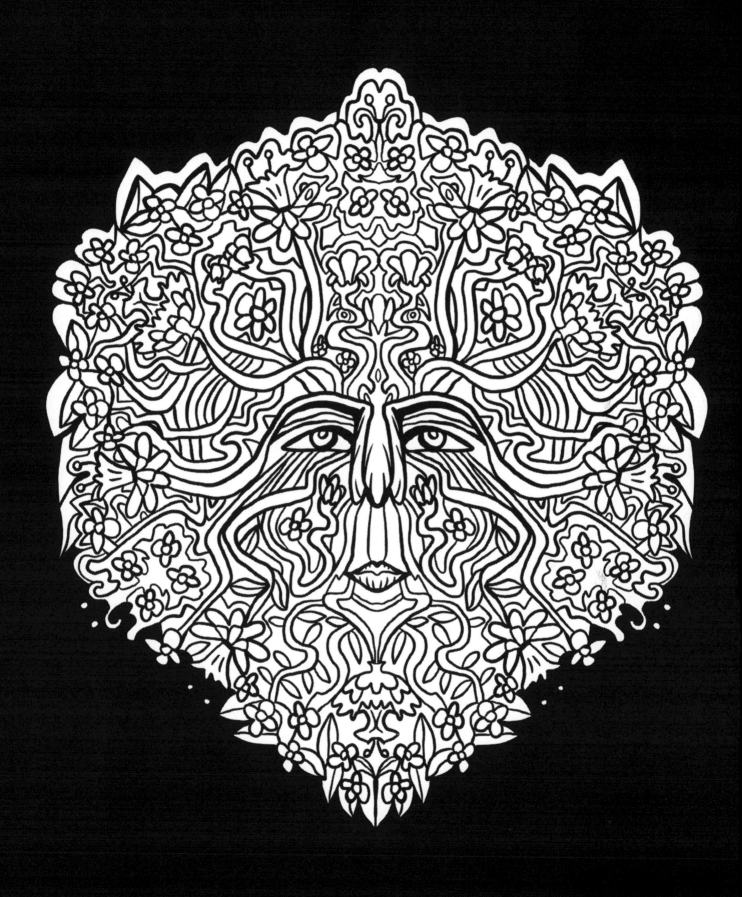

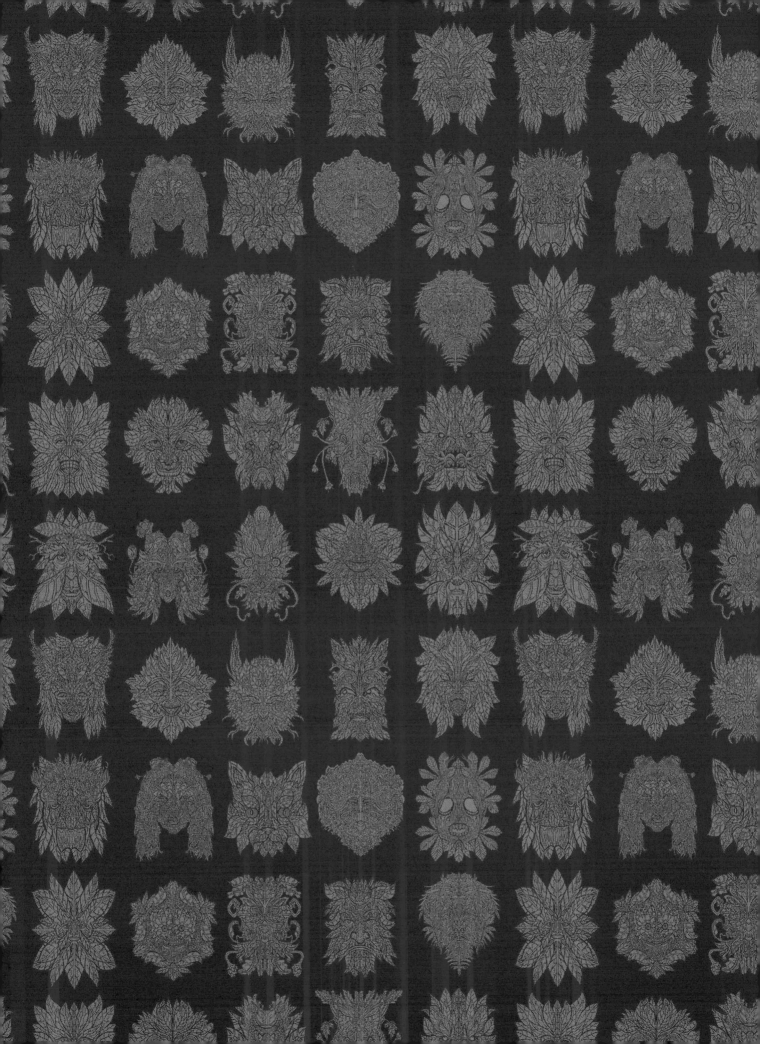

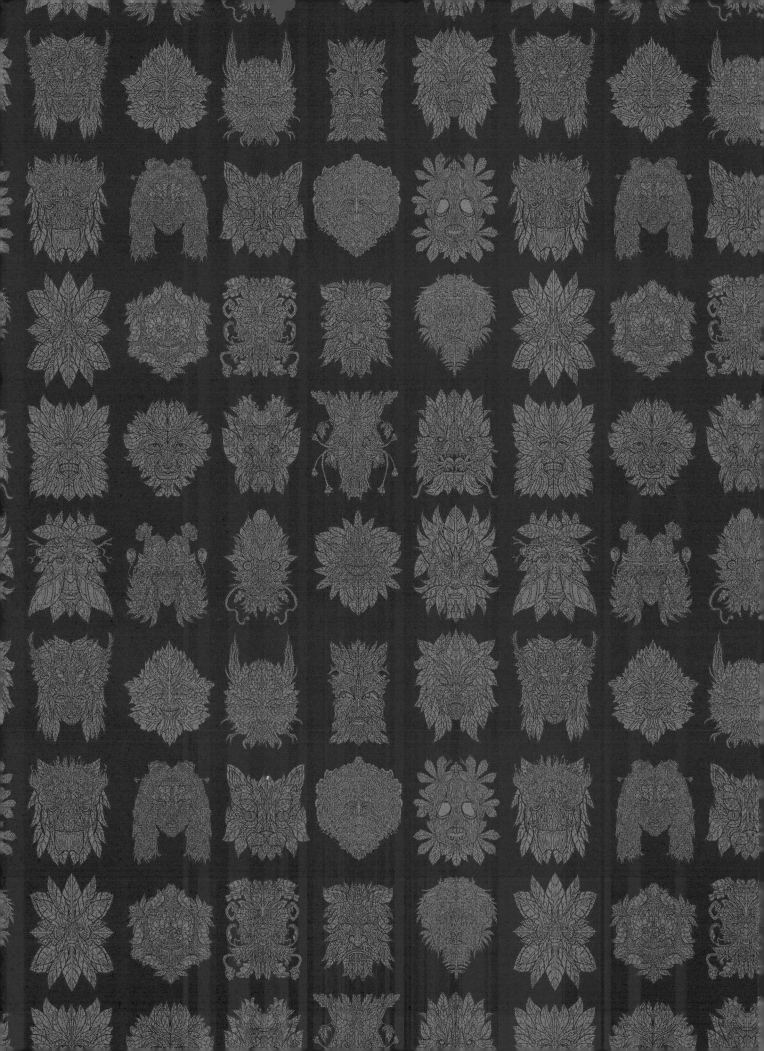

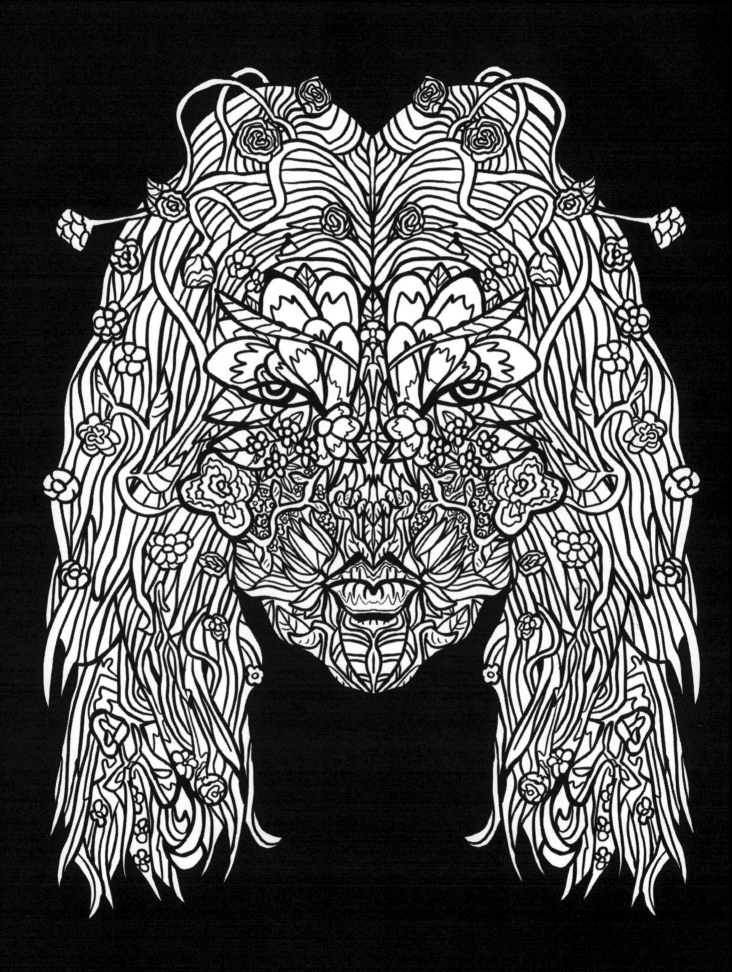

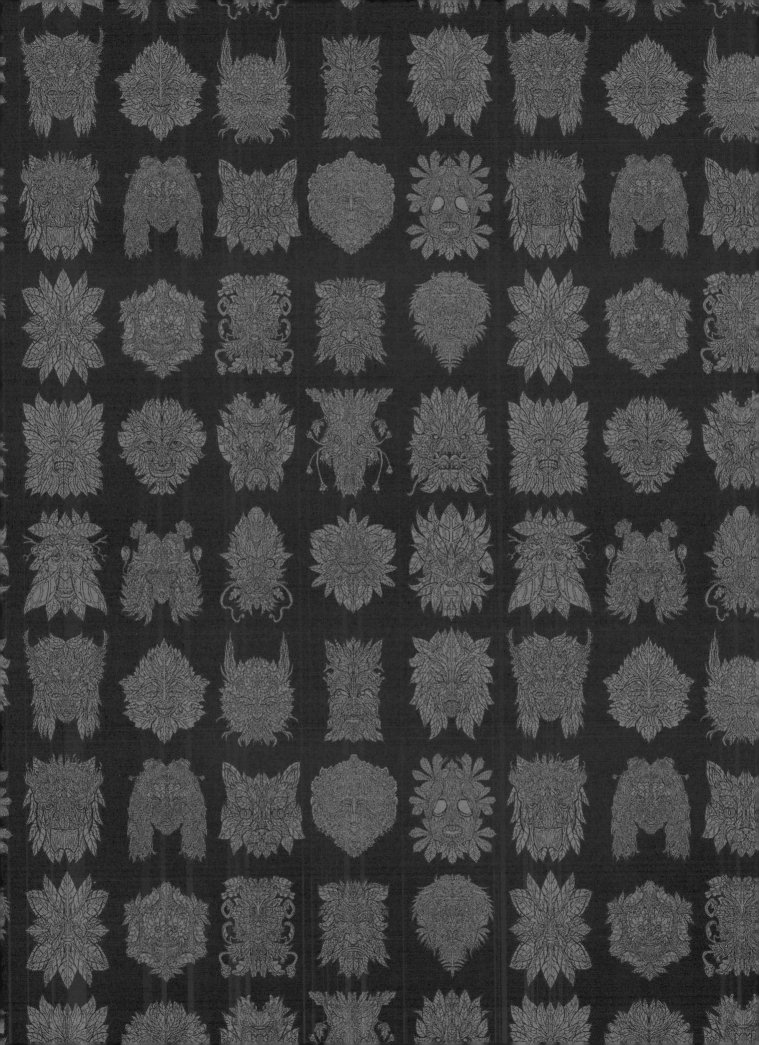

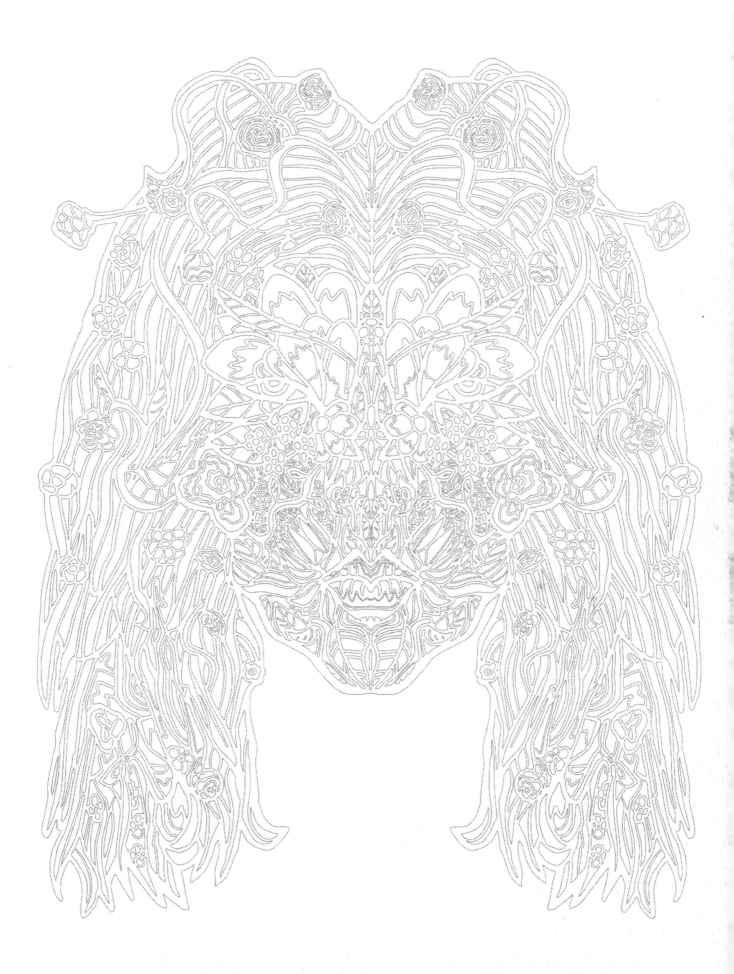

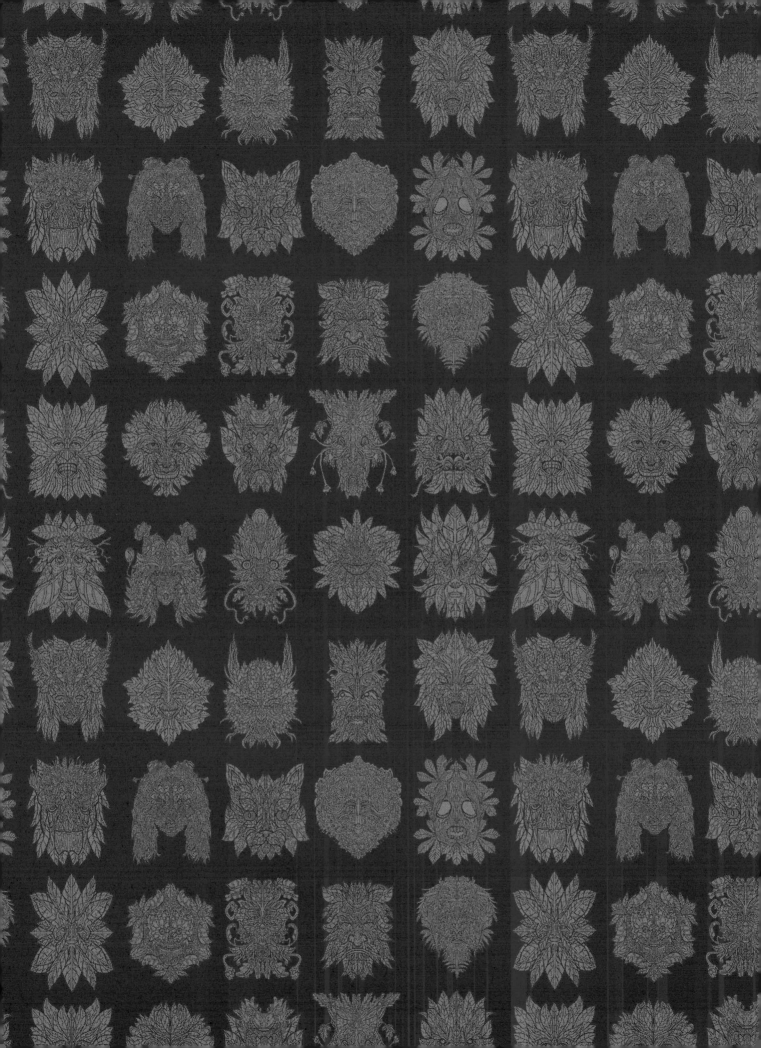

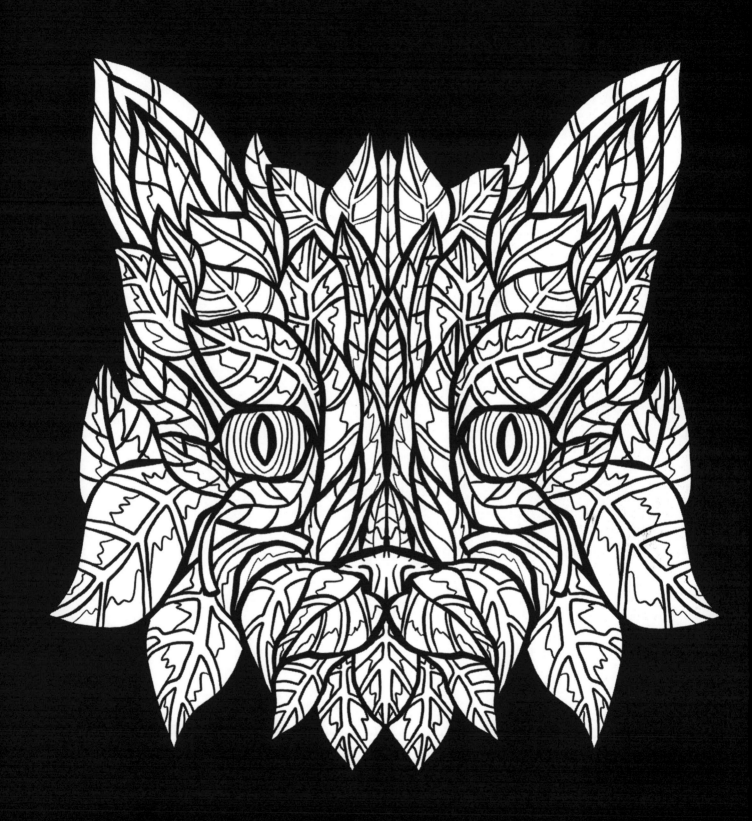

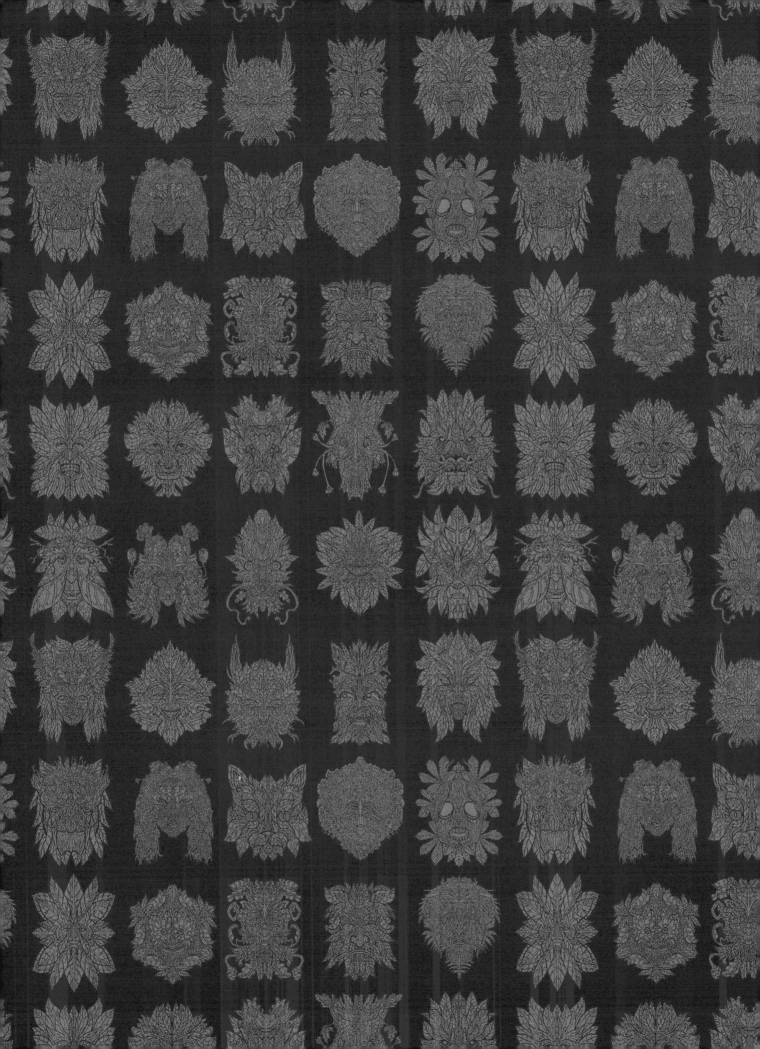

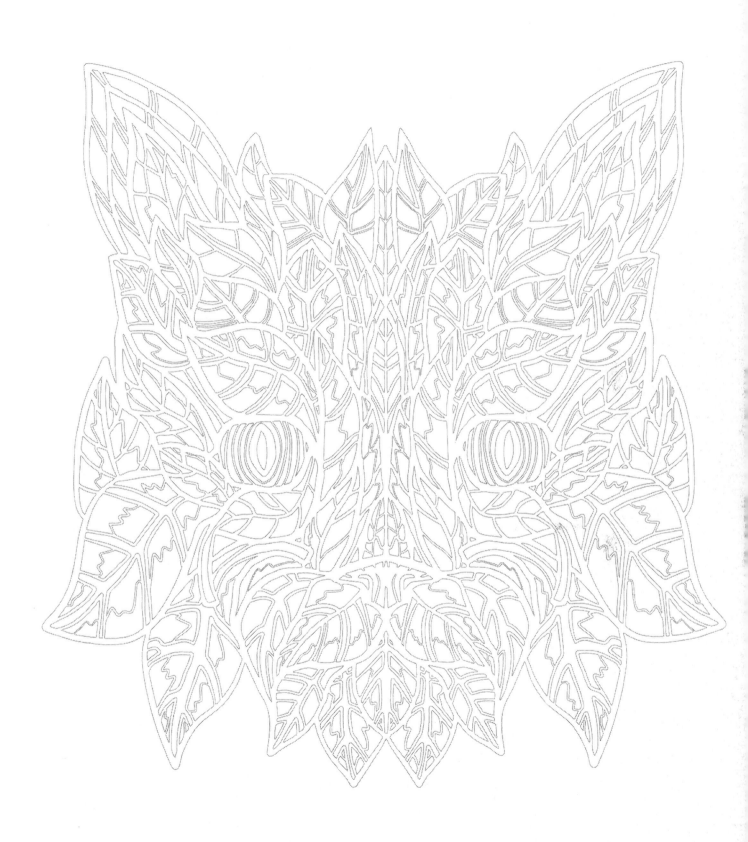

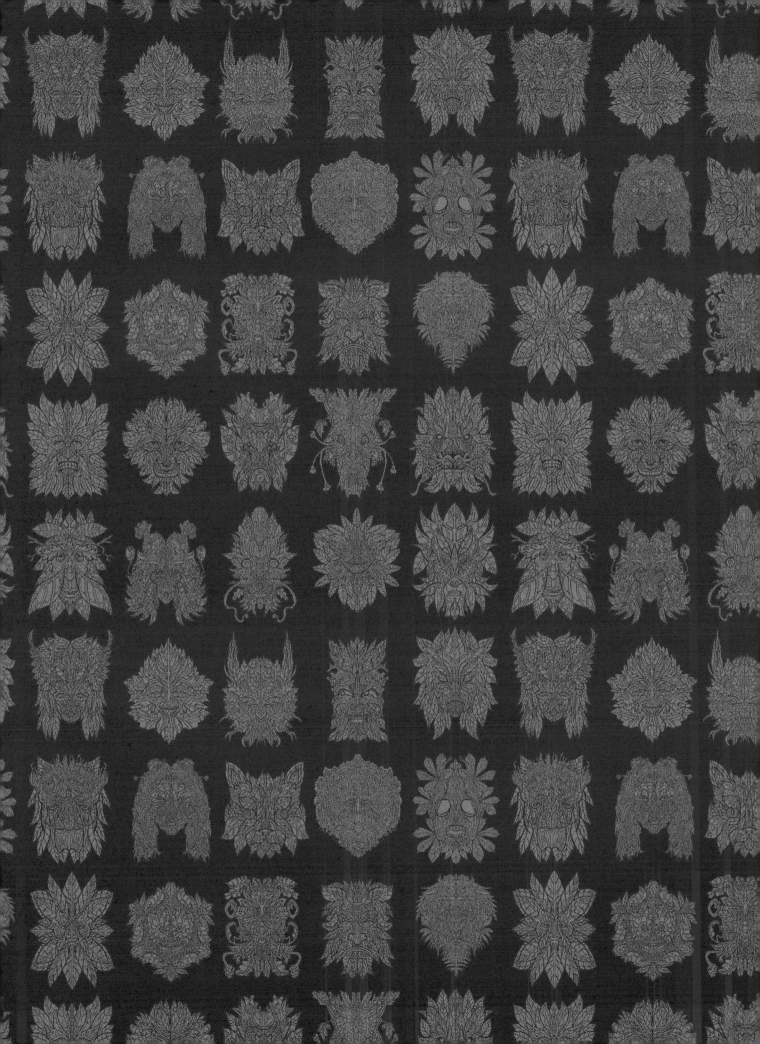

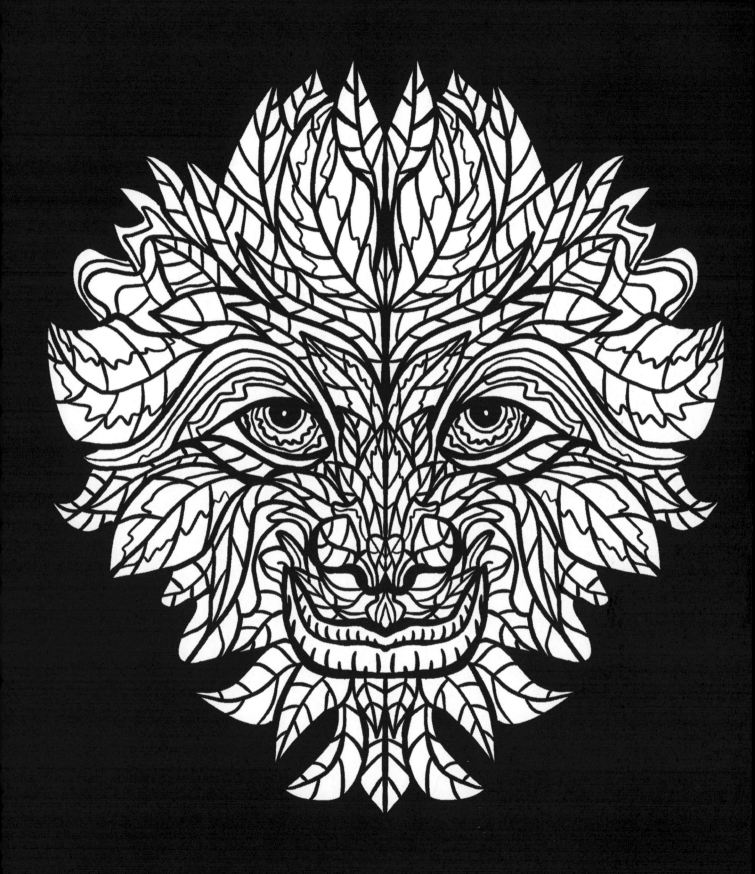

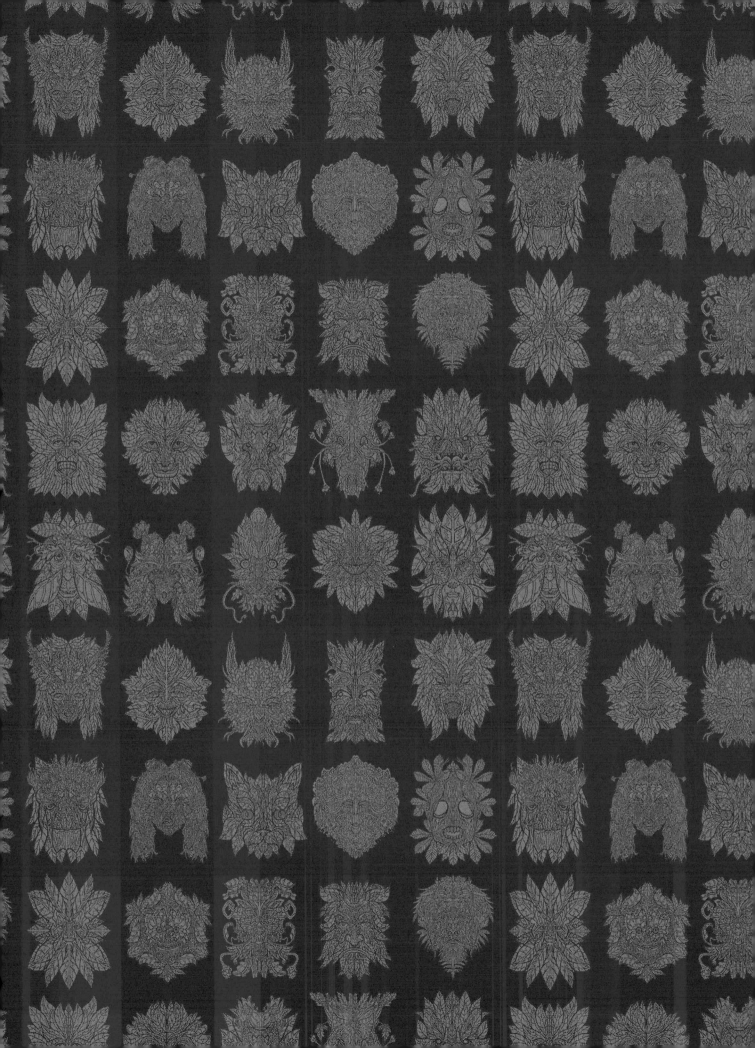

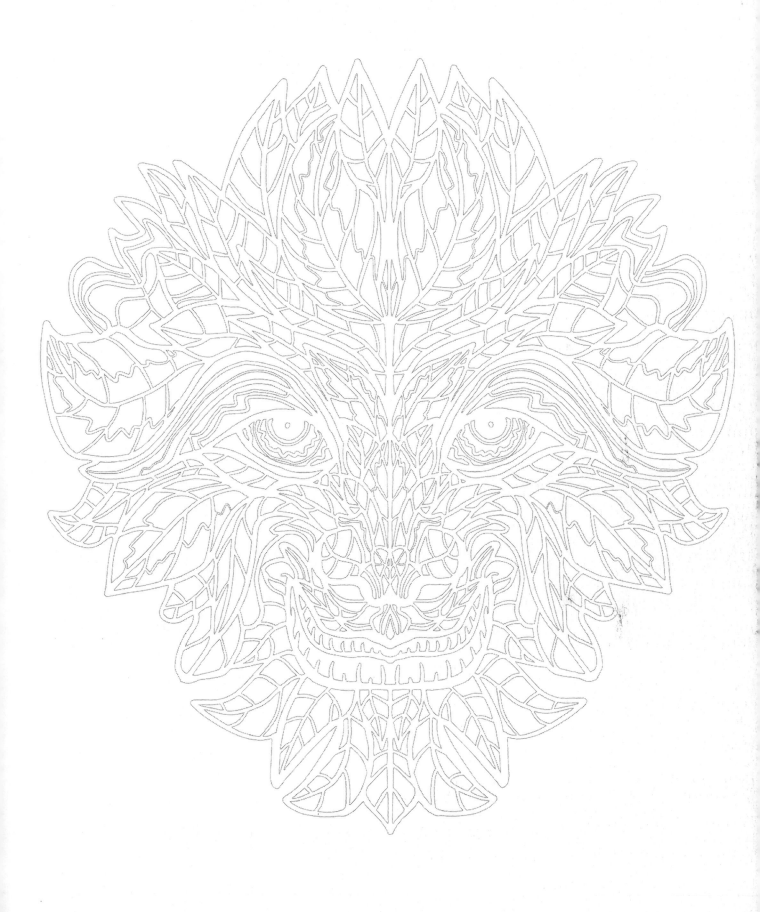

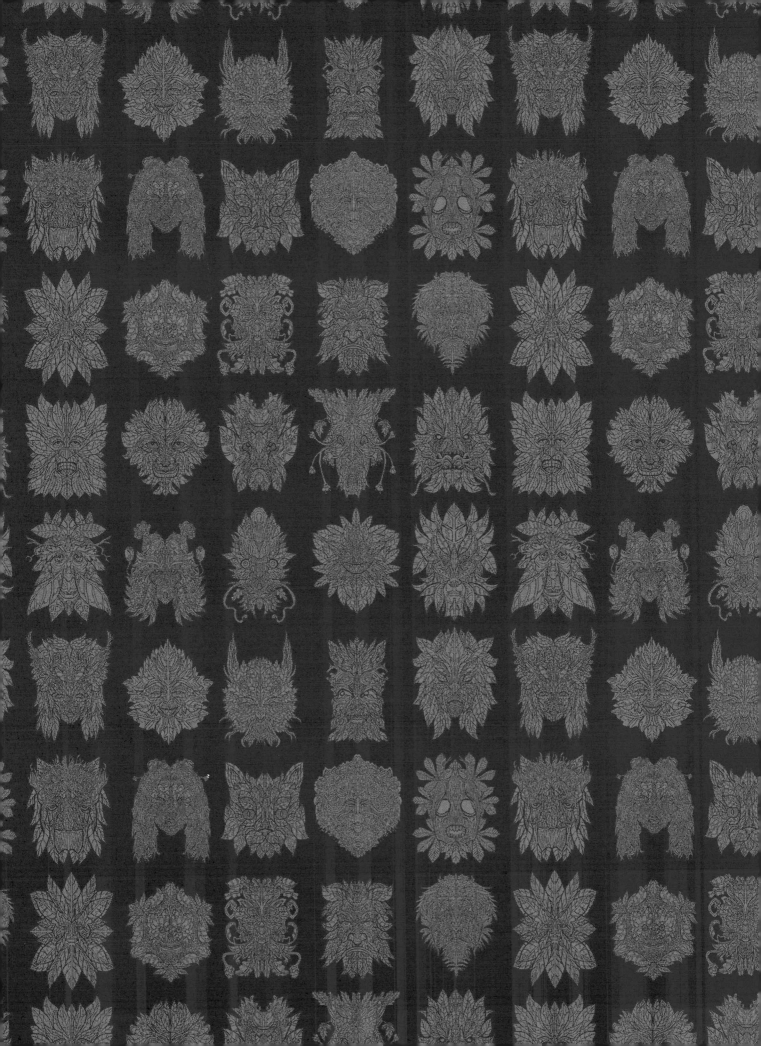

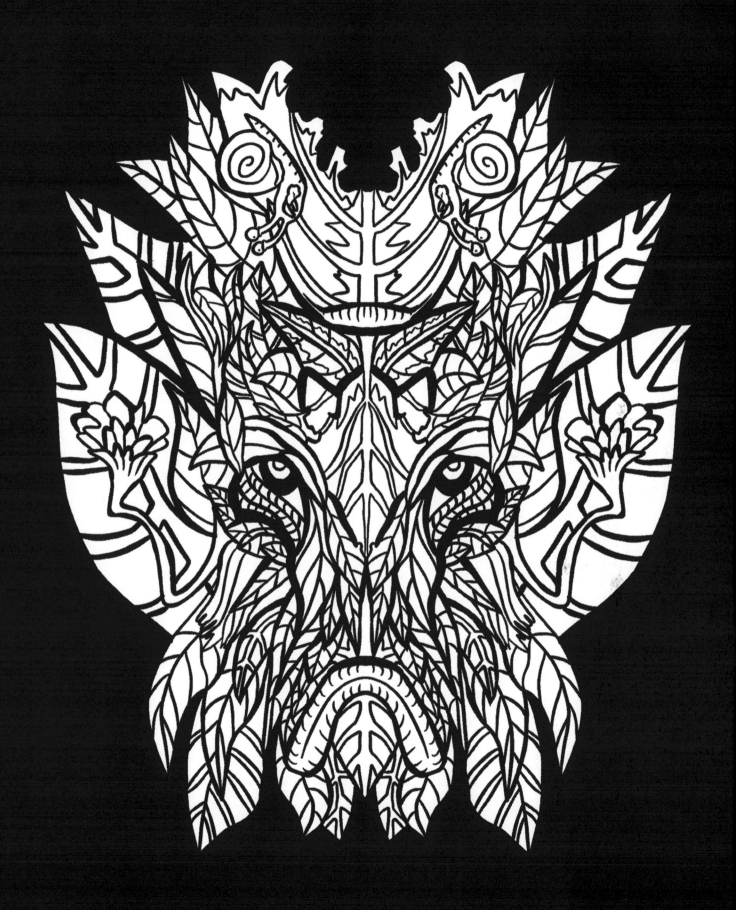

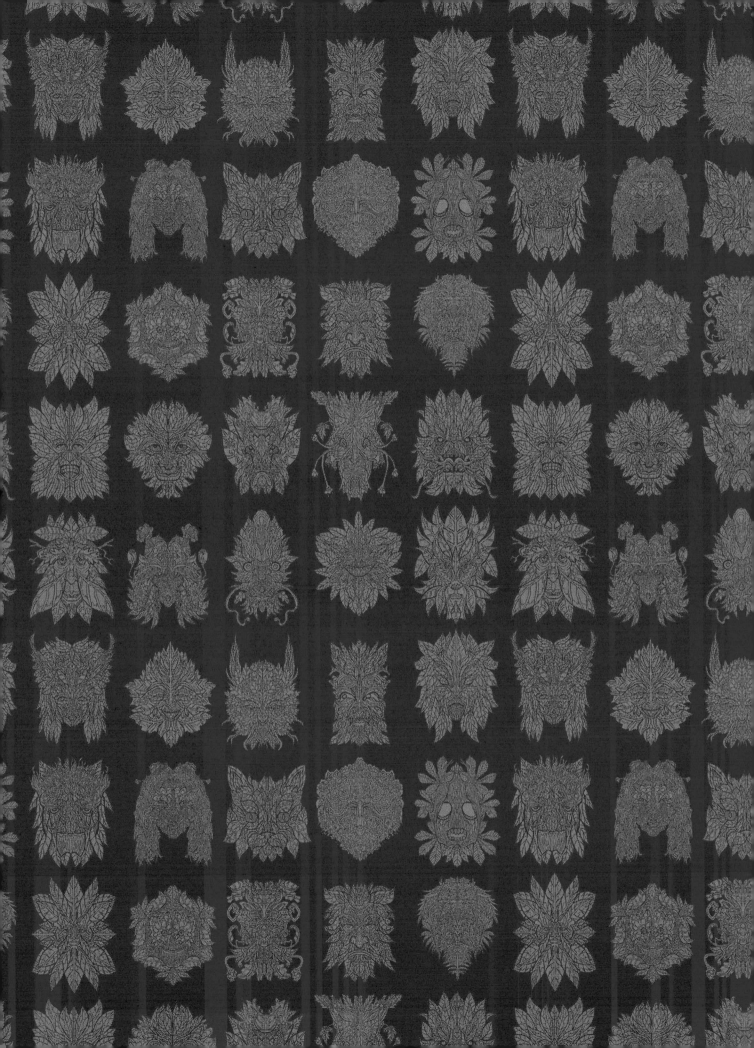

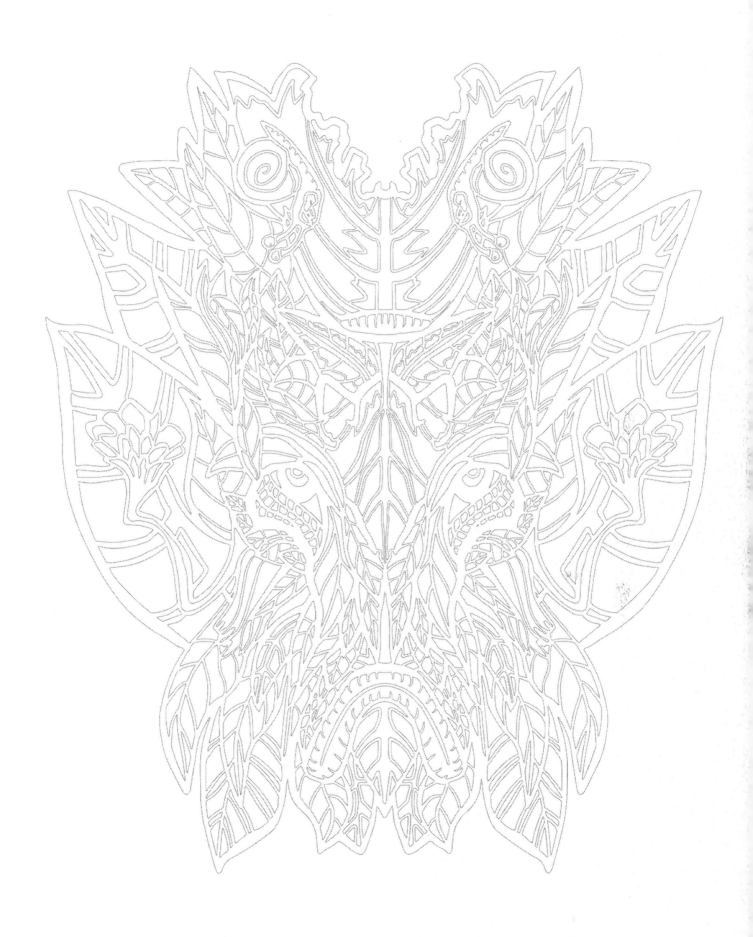

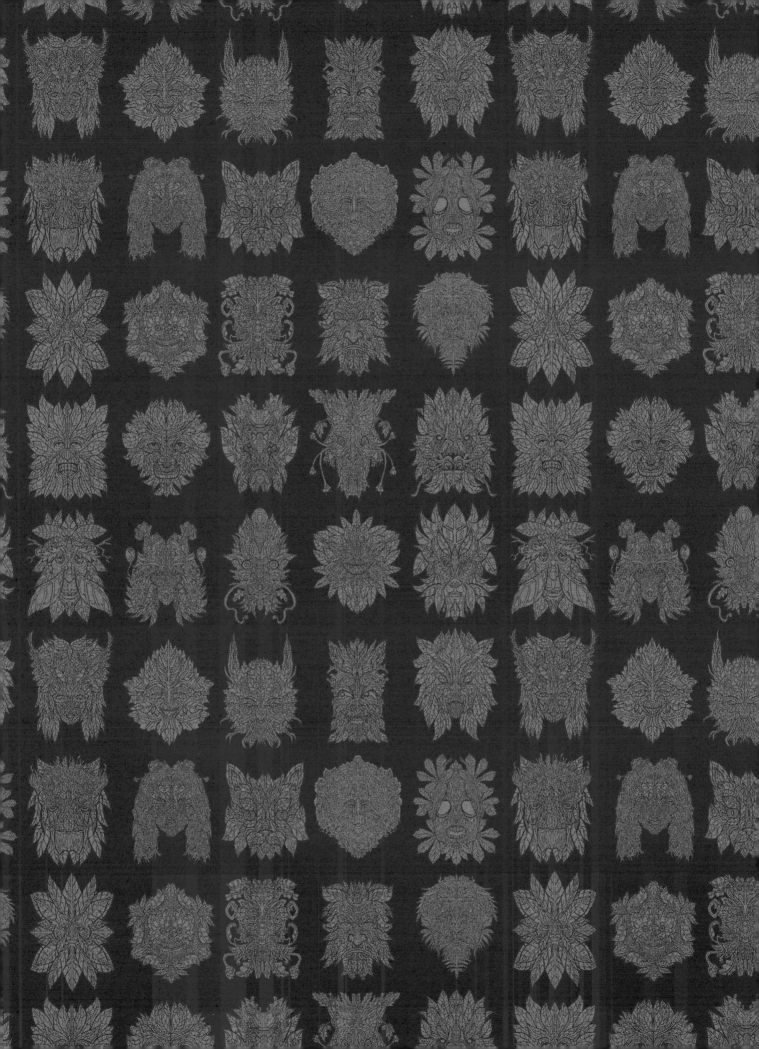

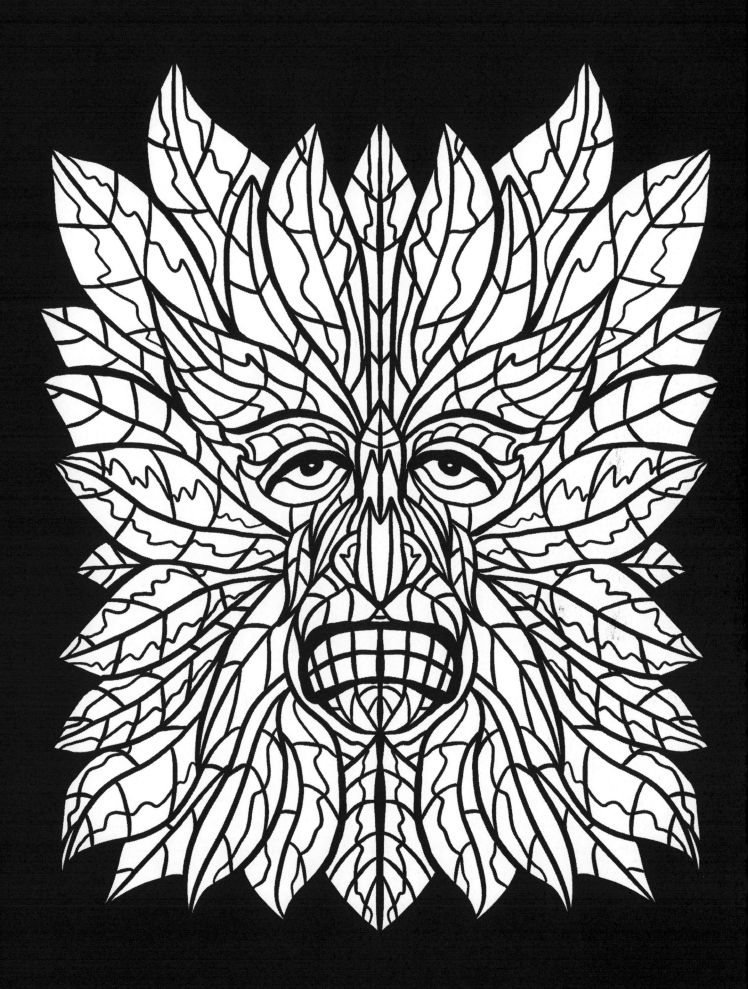

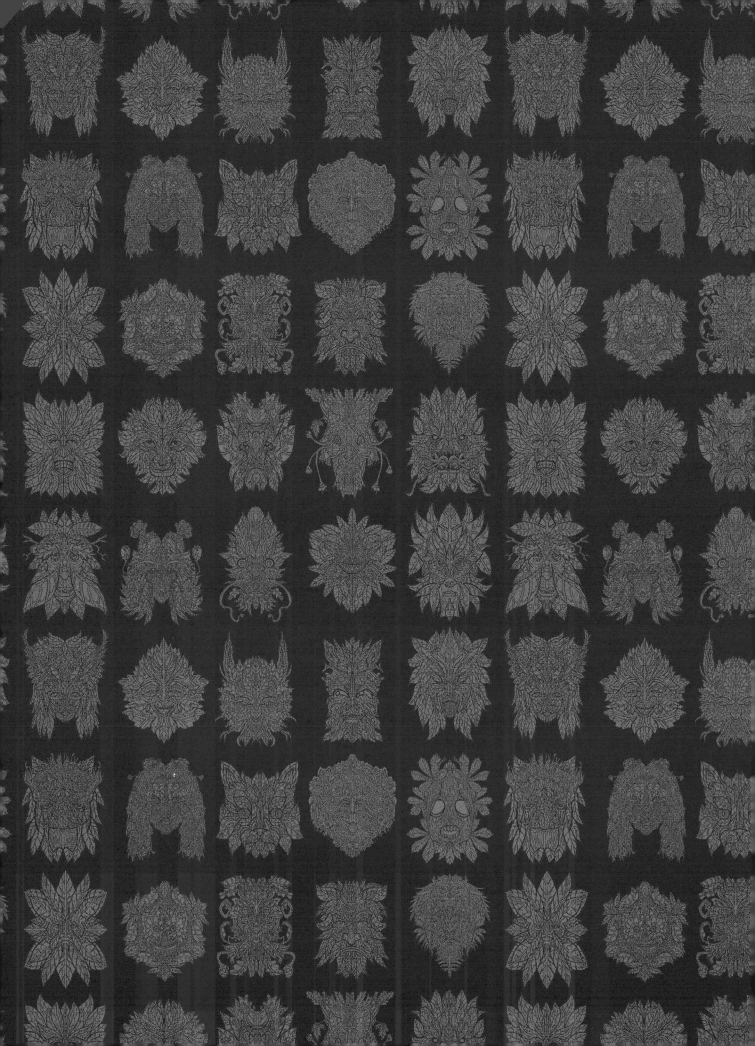

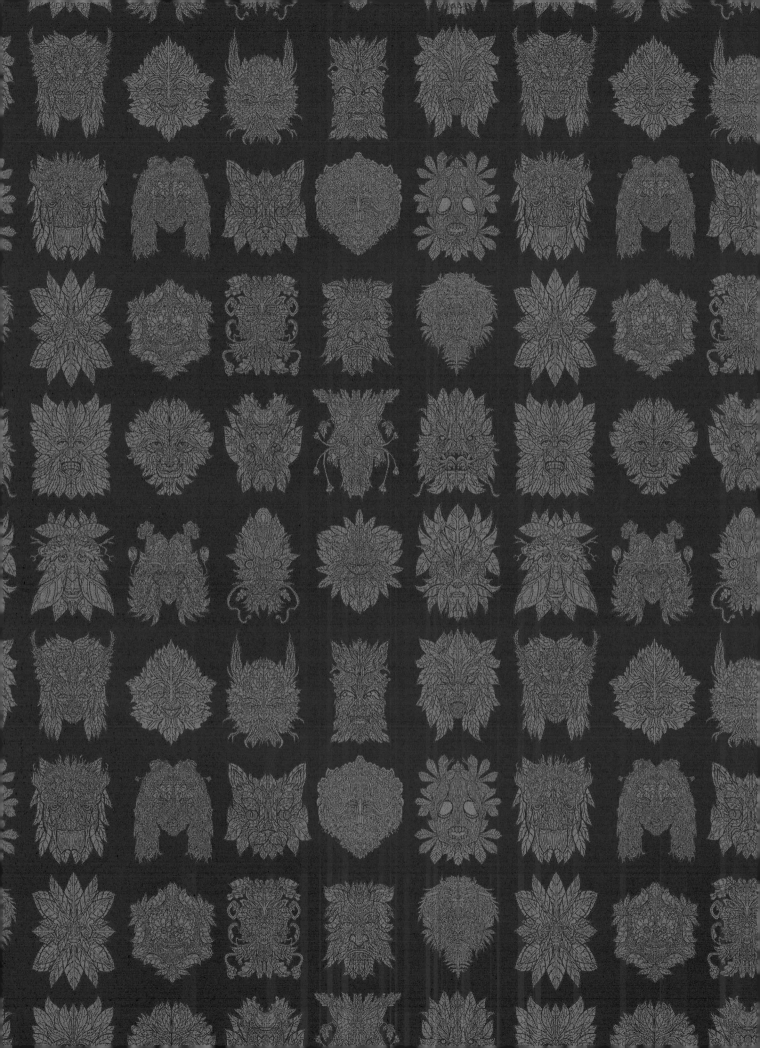

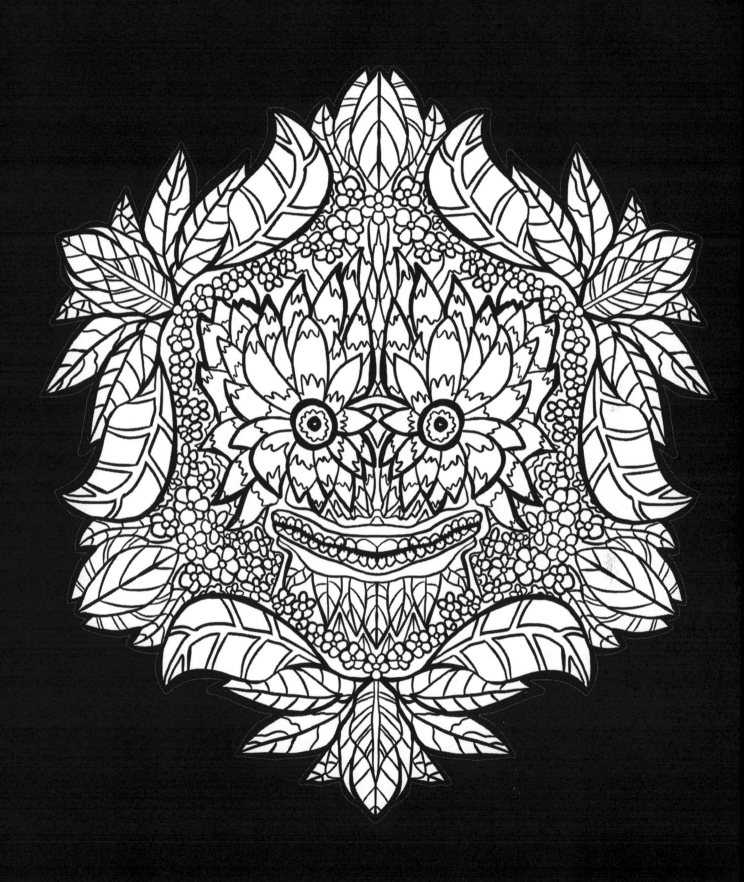

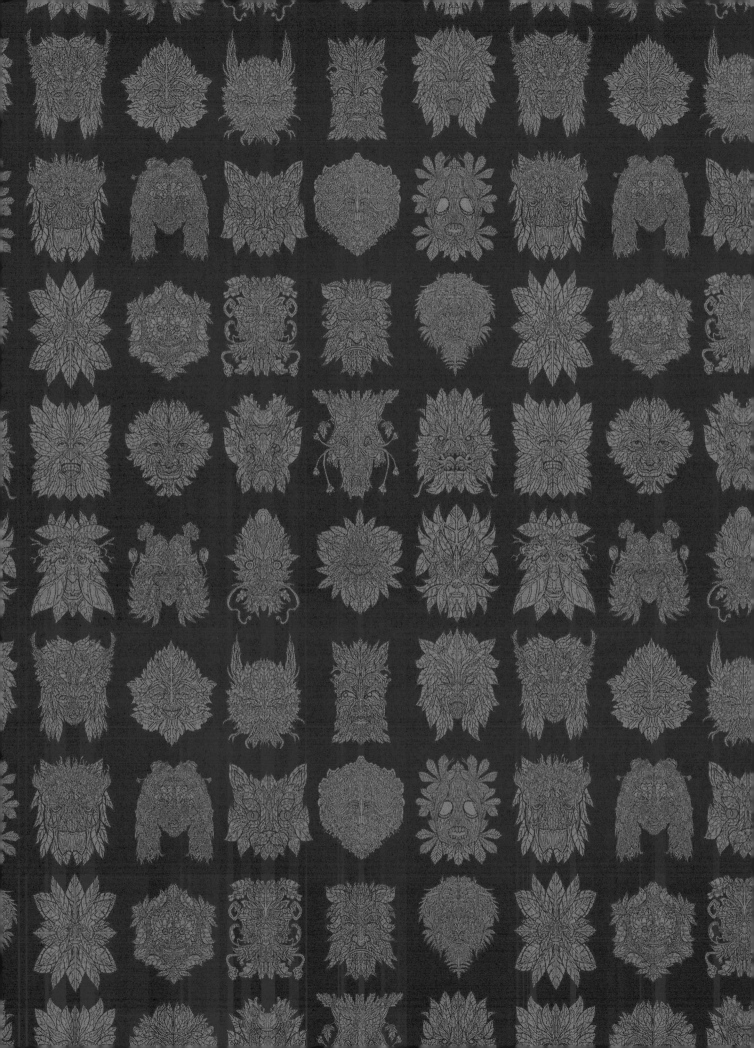

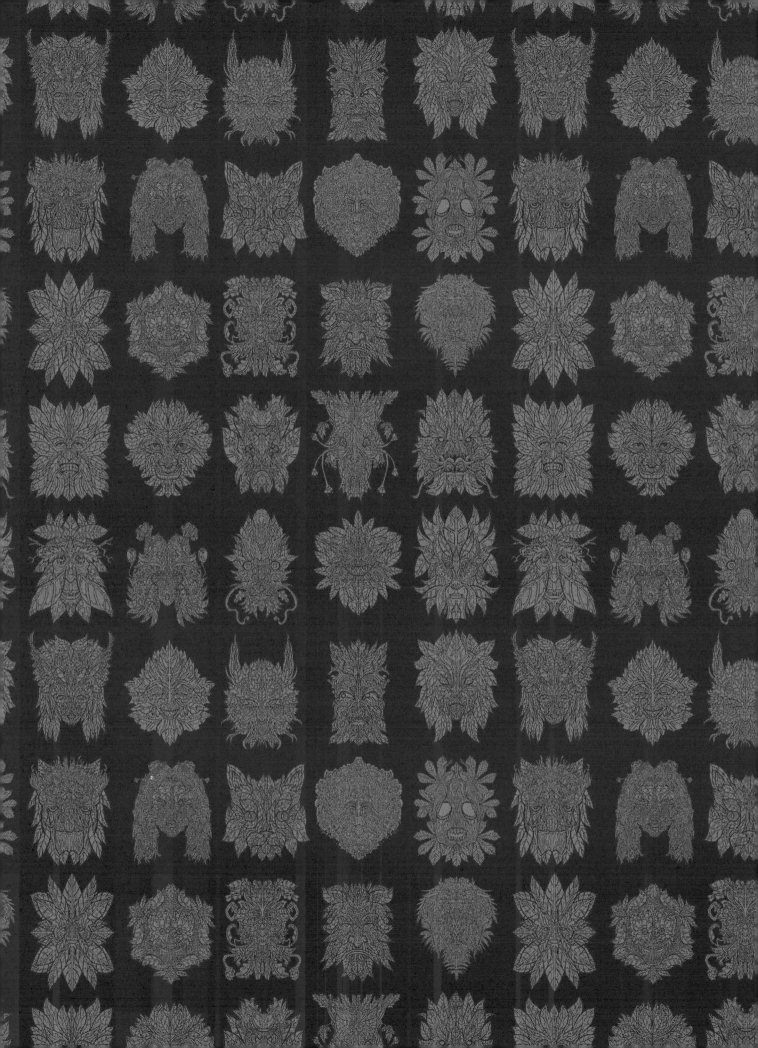

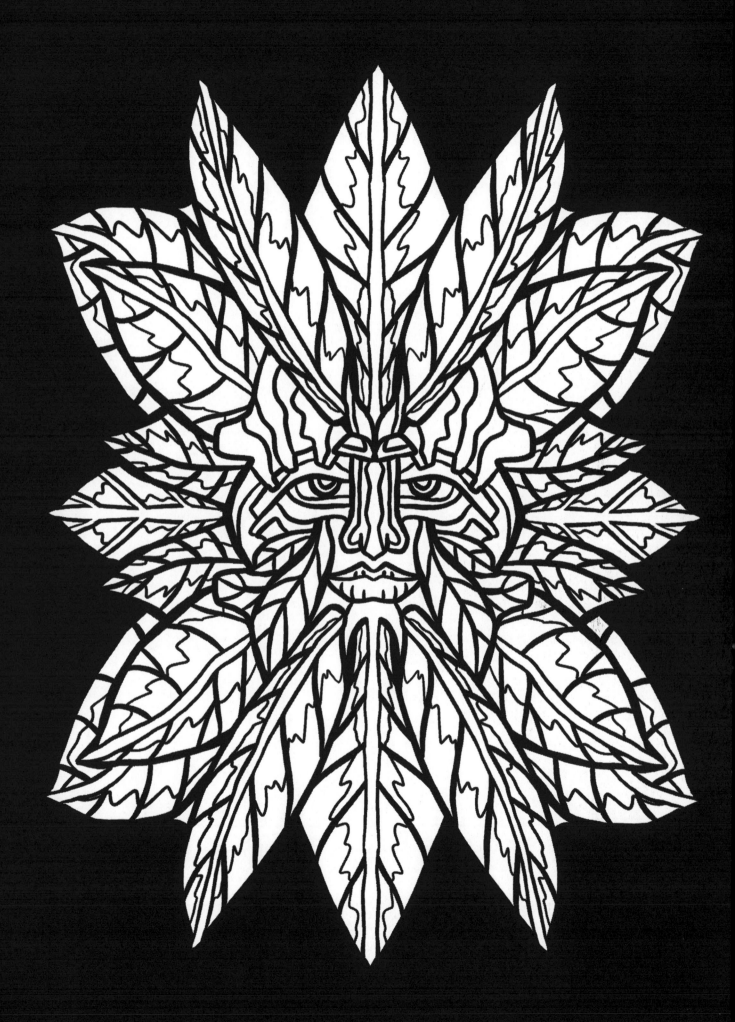

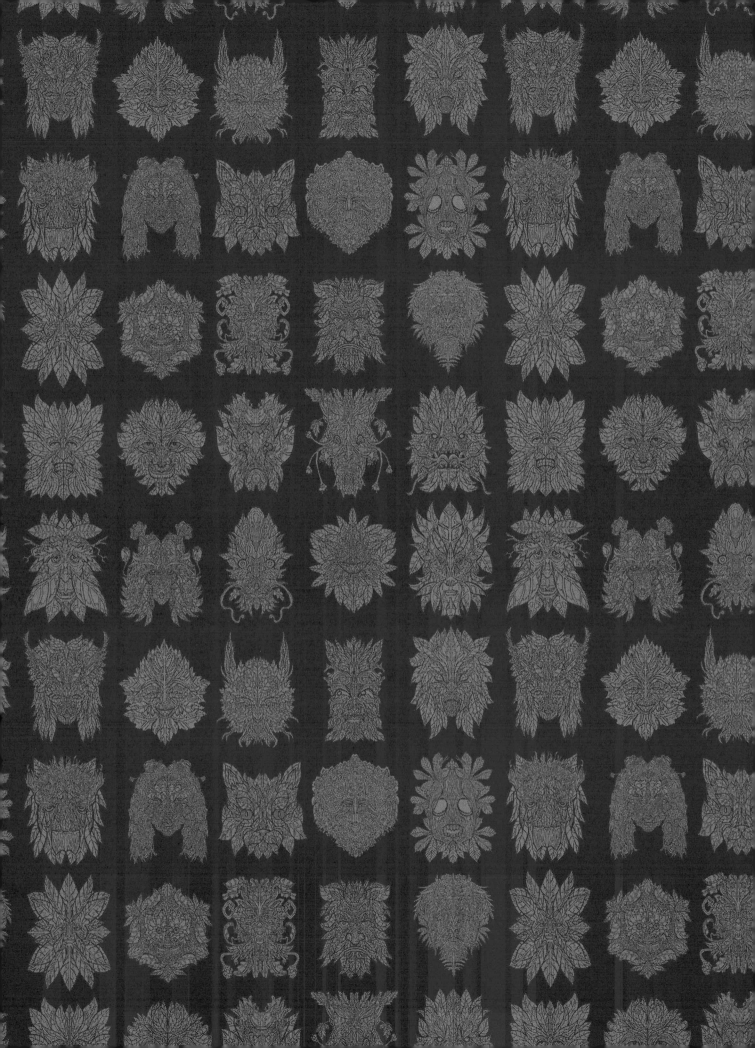

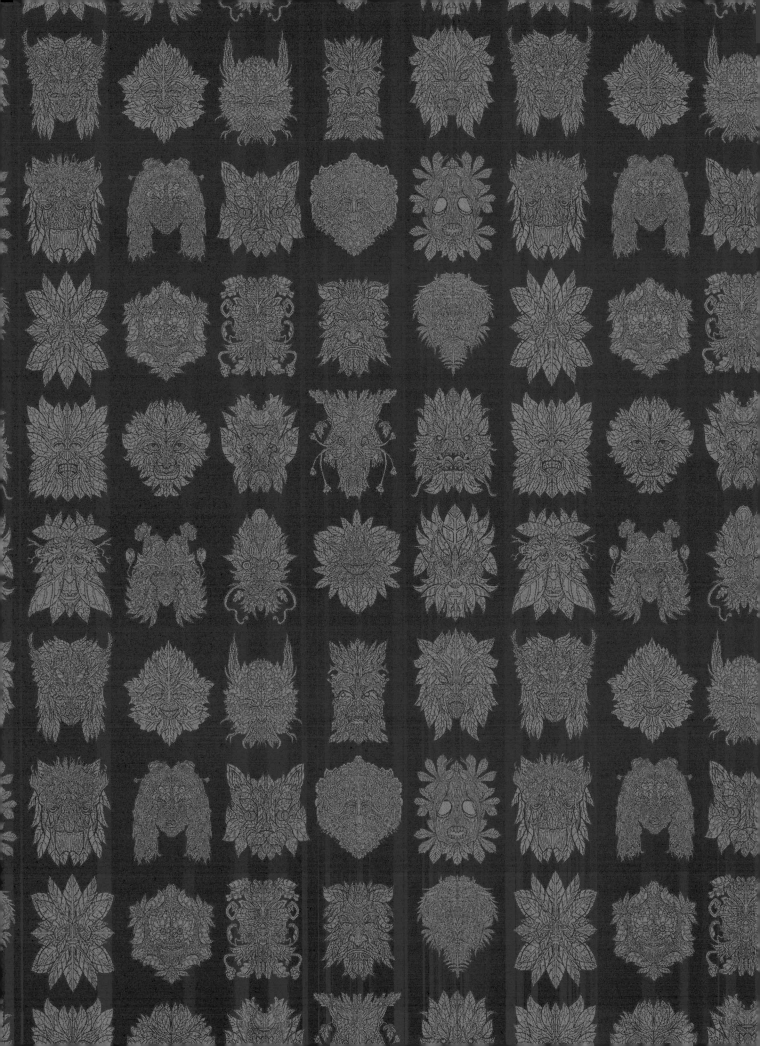

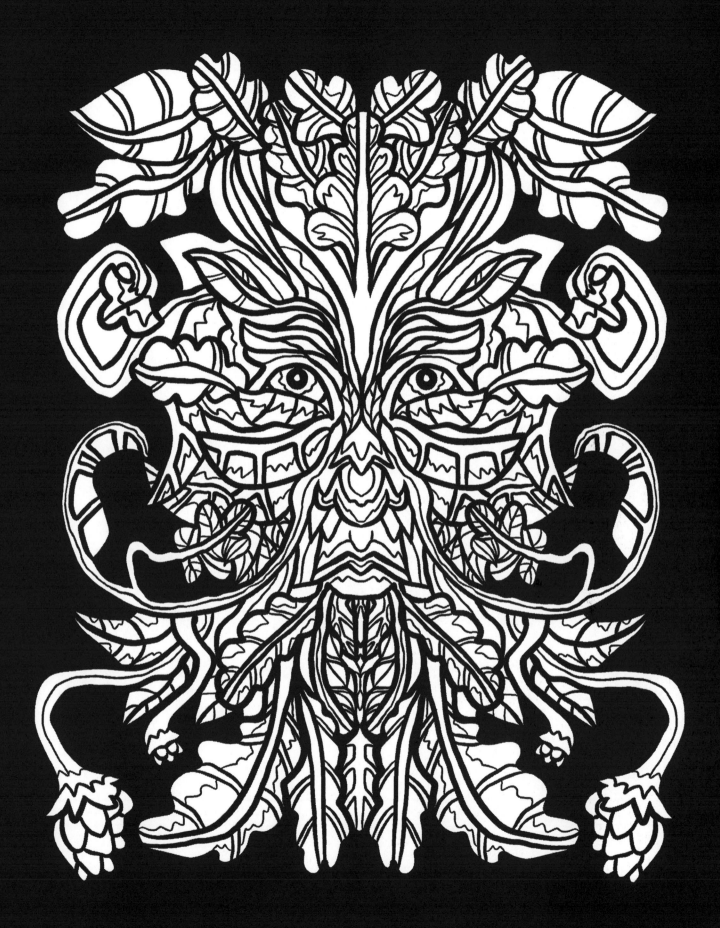

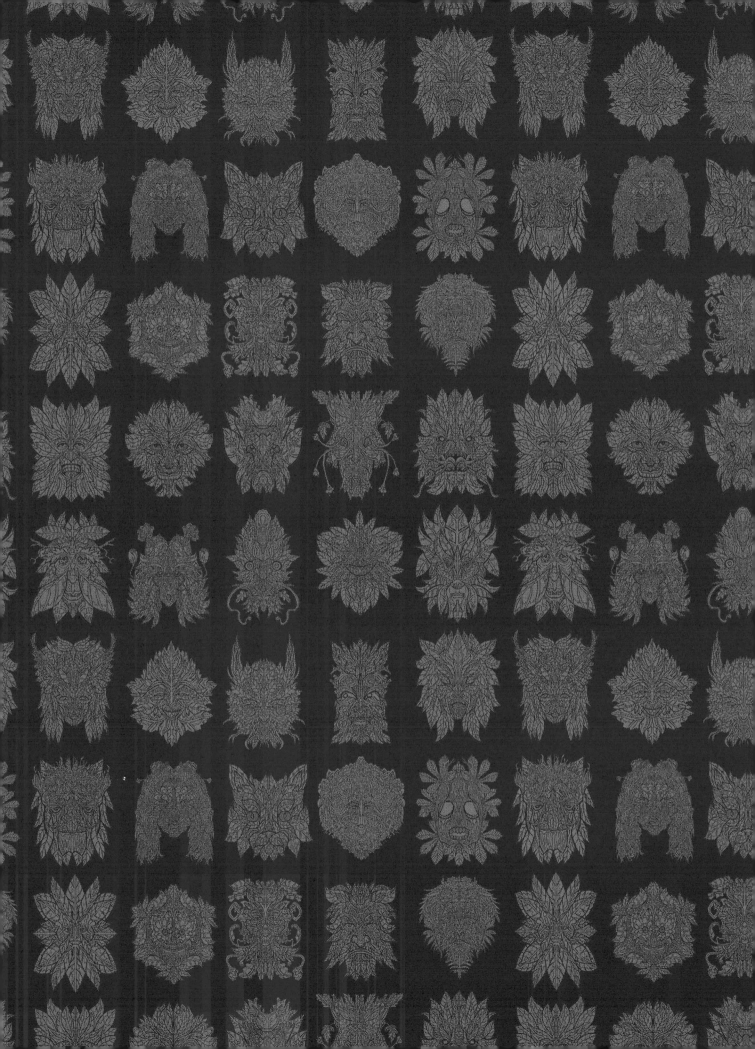

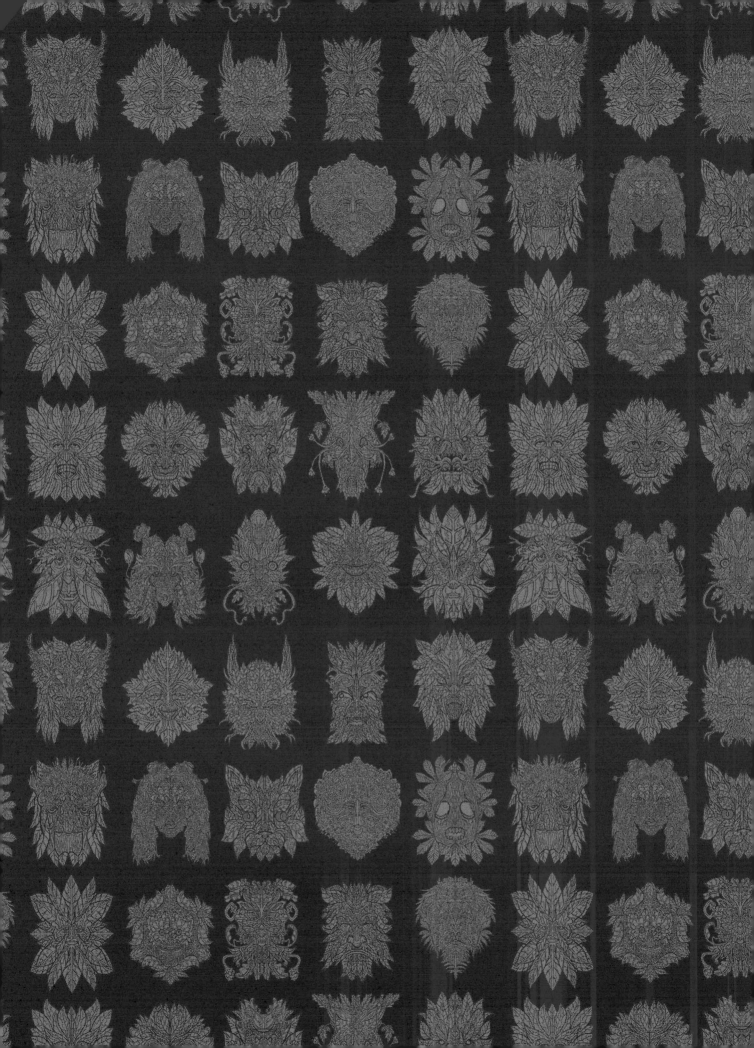

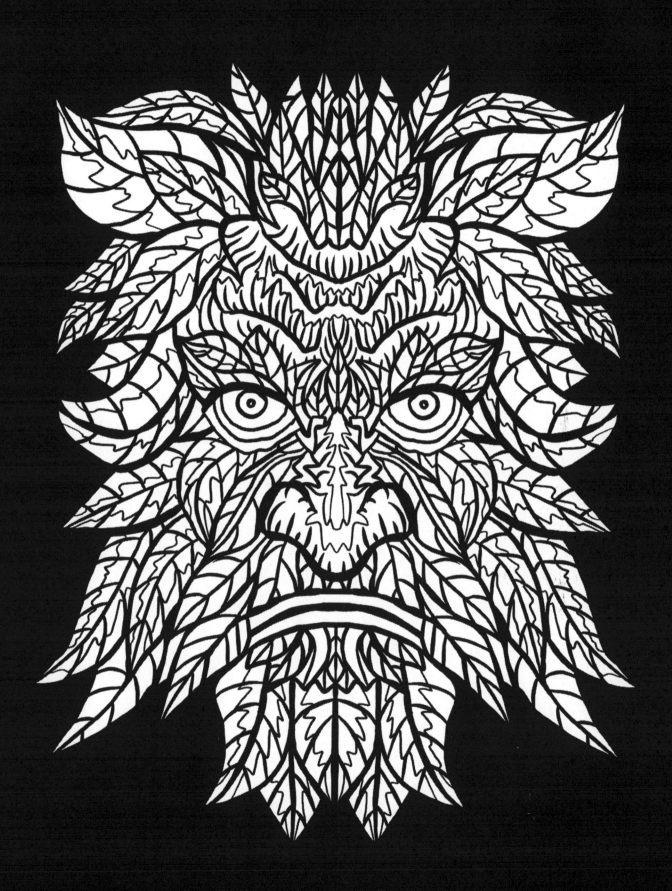

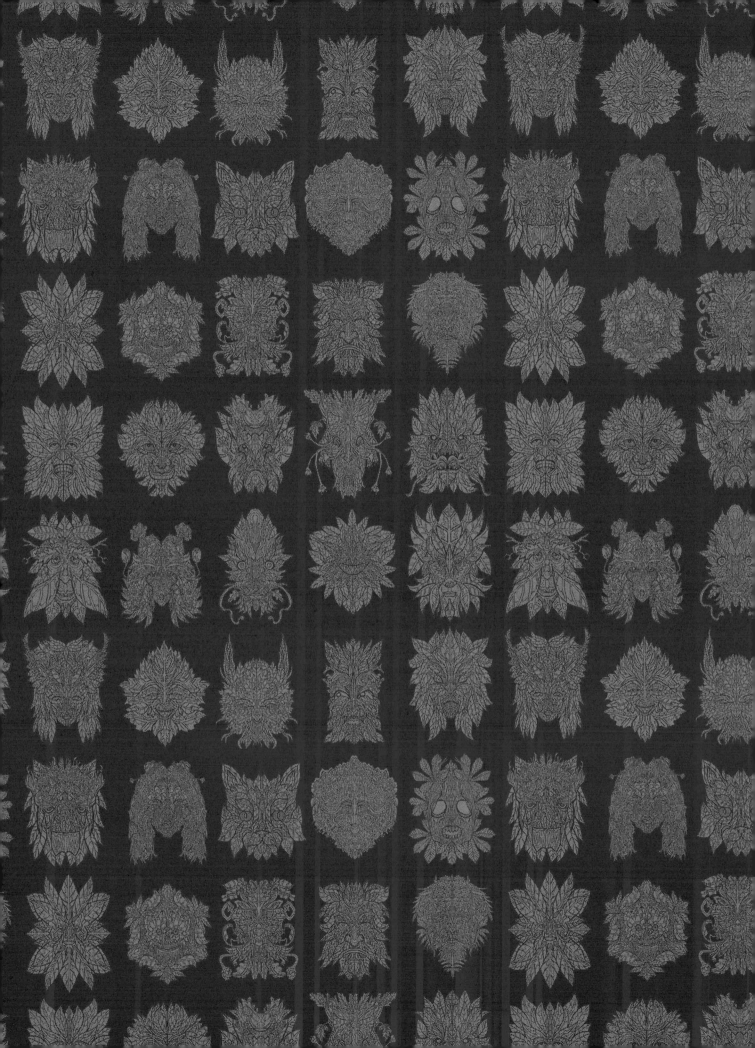

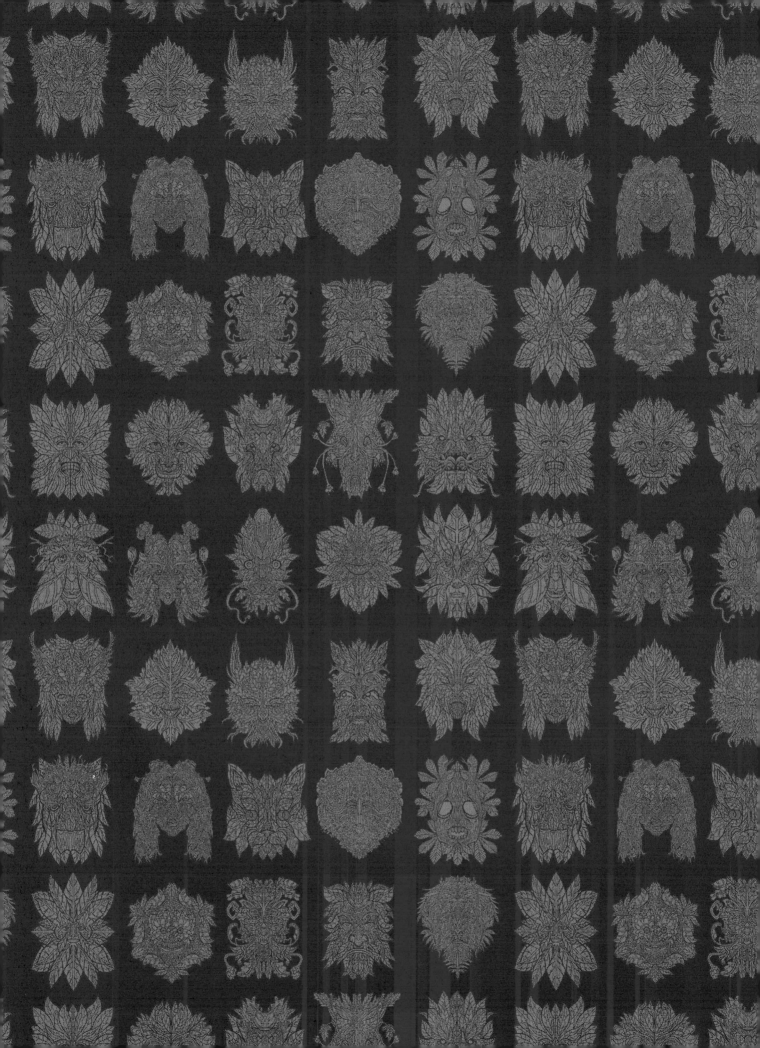

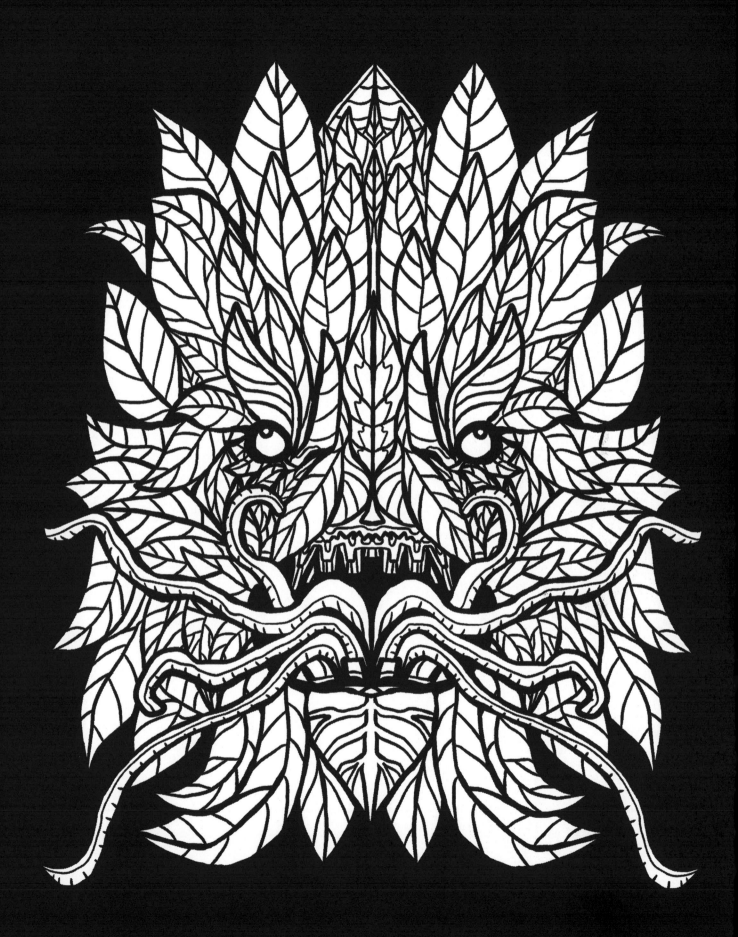

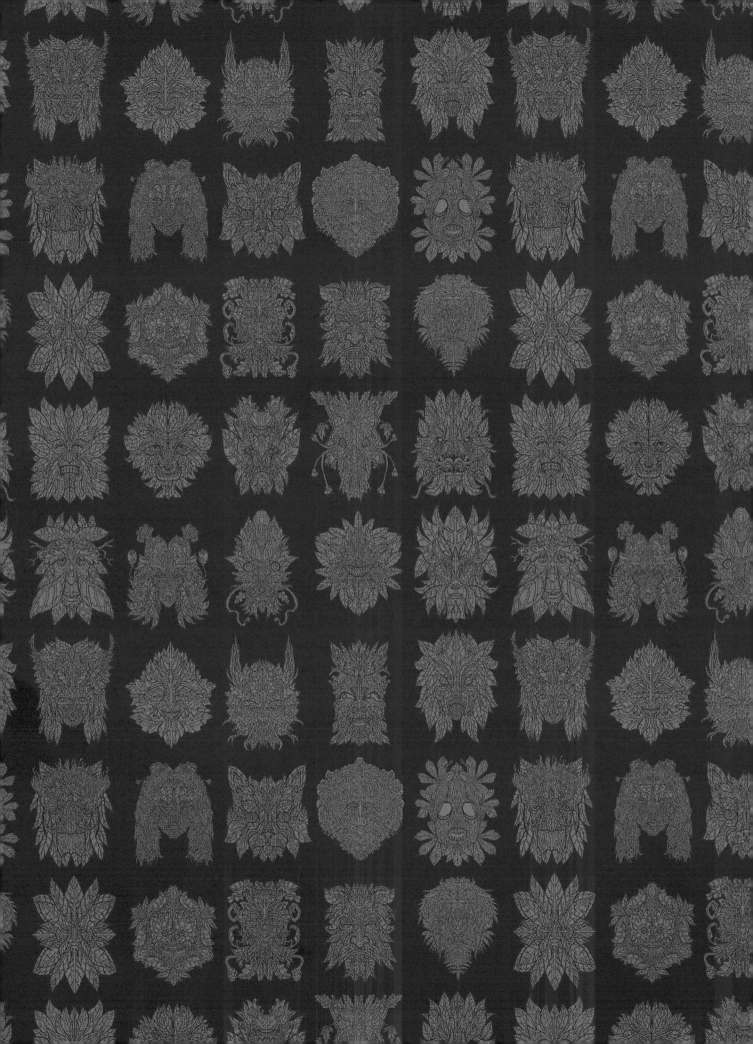

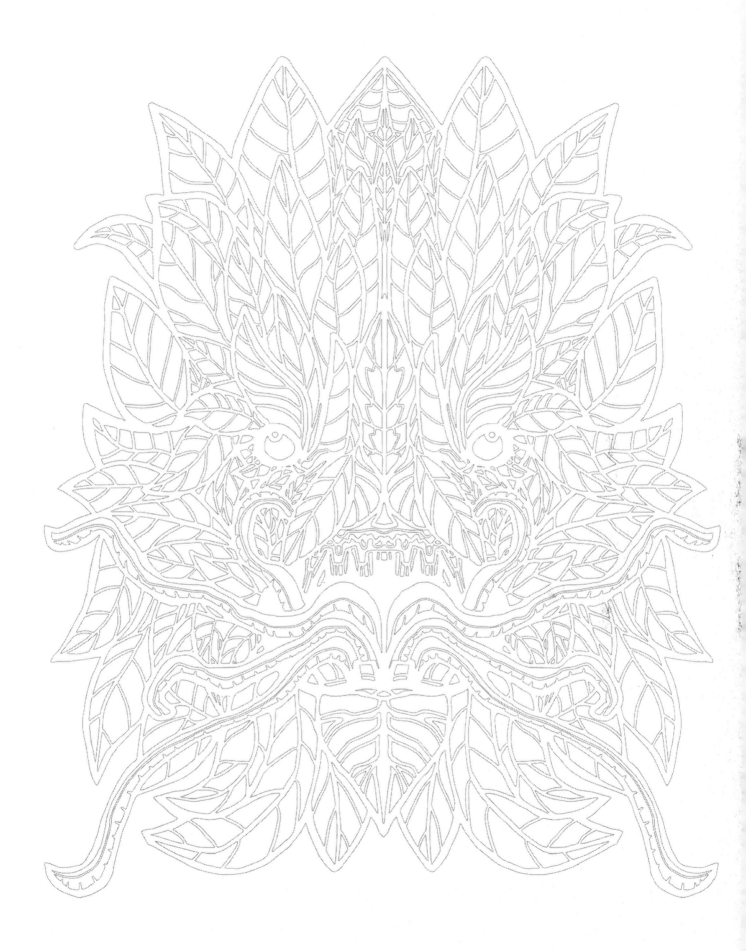

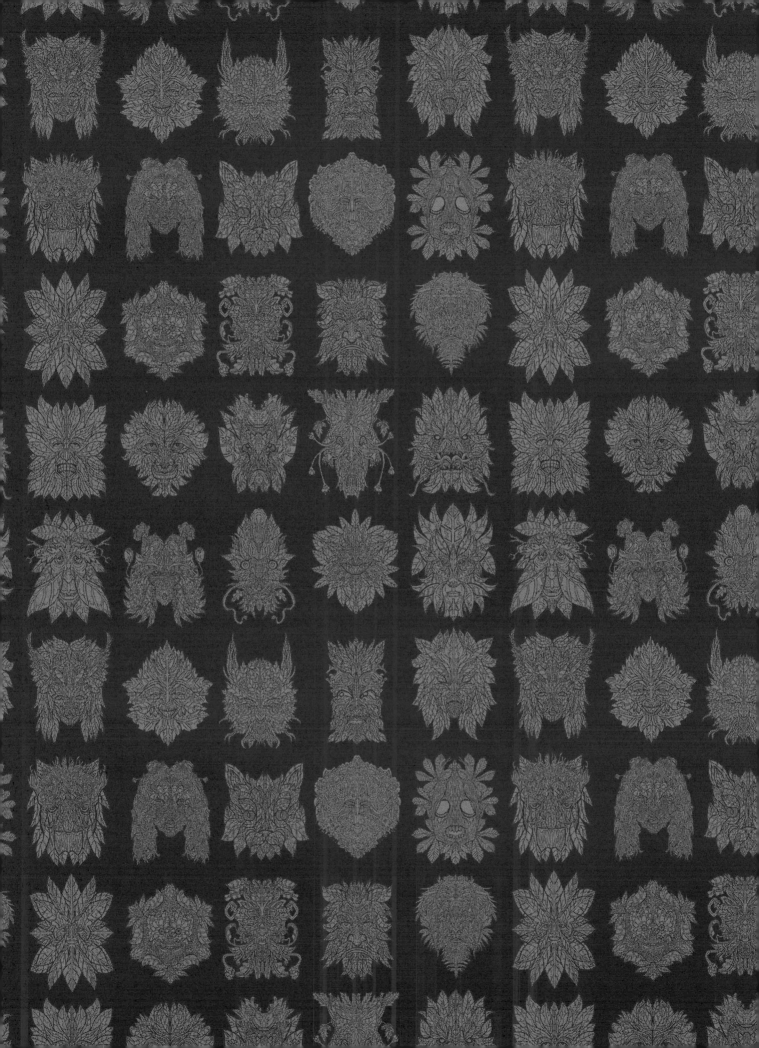

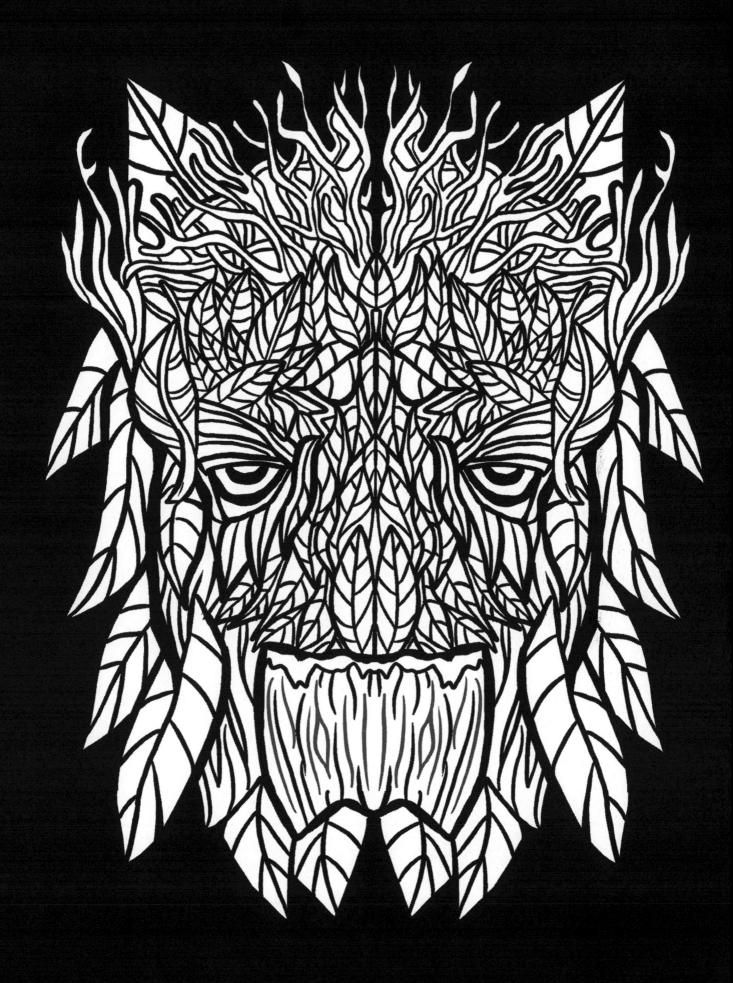

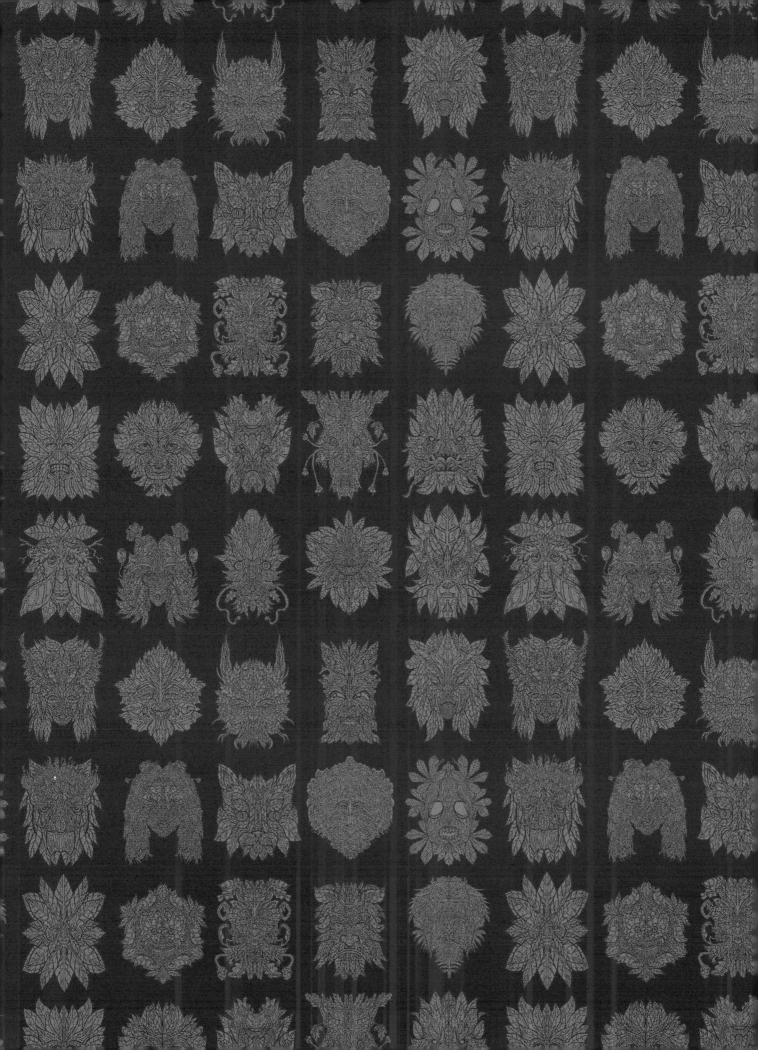

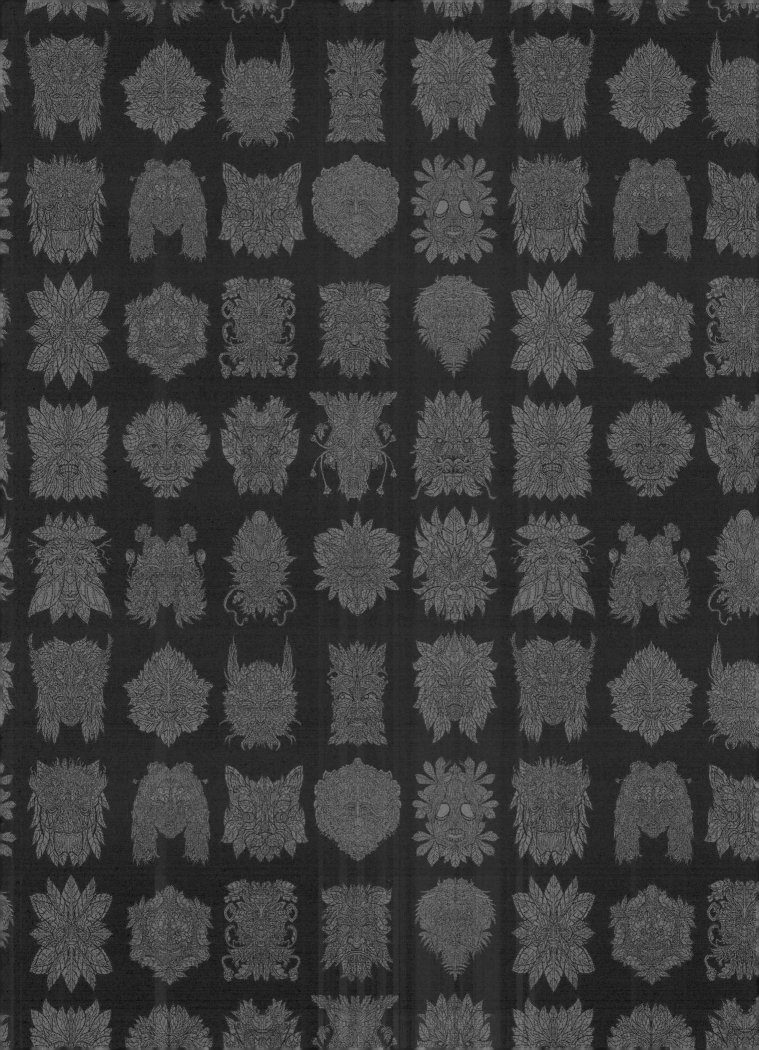

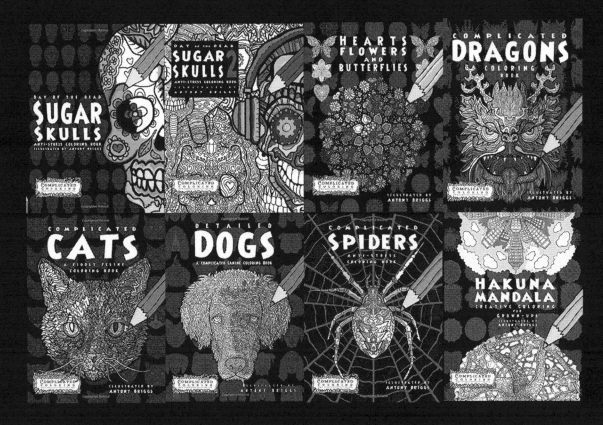

Printed in Poland
by Amazon Fulfillment
Poland Sp. z o.o., Wrocław